Twayne's English Authors Series

Sylvia E. Bowman, *Editor*

INDIANA UNIVERSITY

Lady Isabella Persse Gregory

TEAS 194

Lady Gregory

LADY ISABELLA
PERSSE GREGORY

By EDWARD A. KOPPER, JR.

Slippery Rock State College

TWAYNE PUBLISHERS

A DIVISION OF G. K. HALL & CO., BOSTON

Library of Congress Cataloging in Publication Data

Kopper, Edward A
  Lady Isabella Persse Gregory.

  (Twayne's English authors series; TEAS 194)
  Bibliography: p. 151–56.
  Includes index.
  1.   Gregory, Isabella Augusta Persse, Lady, 1852–1932.
PR4728.G5Z63   822'.9'12 [B]   76-24845
ISBN 0-8057-6658-8

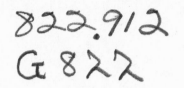

To
Peg, Eddie, and Kevin

Contents

About the Author

Dr. Edward A. Kopper, Jr. is a James Joyce scholar of international reputation and has published widely on such writers as Joyce, Lawrence Durrell, Graham Greene, and Gerard Manley Hopkins. He is one of the few Joyceans to publish significantly on both *Ulysses* and *Finnegans Wake*. For example, two of Dr. Kopper's better known studies include an analysis of comedy in *Ulysses*, which appeared in *Mosaic* (Fall 1972), and a chapter on the Tavern Feast in *Finnegans Wake*, in *A Conceptual Guide to Finnegans Wake* (Penn State Press, 1974). Presently, Dr. Kopper is editor of *The Modern British Literature Newsletter*, a biannual journal.

Dr. Kopper has headed a number of literary panels at national meetings, including service as chairman of the James Joyce section of NEMLA. In 1973, he read a paper on Bloom and Earwicker at the International James Joyce Symposium in Dublin. Dr. Kopper has also given TV lectures on Joyce and D. H. Lawrence.

In 1973, Dr. Kopper was chosen outstanding professor by the students of Slippery Rock State College and, in 1974, distinguished professor of humanities and fine arts and teacher laureate. In 1975, he was named distinguished professor of English by the Commonwealth of Pennsylvania. Before coming to Slippery Rock, Dr. Kopper taught at Temple University, Villanova University, and Indiana University at South Bend. He also served for a time as chairman of English at Slippery Rock and is now graduate coordinator of English.

Dr. Kopper received his B.S. from St. Joseph's College (Philadelphia) and his M.A. and Ph.D. from Temple University.

Preface

This study proposes to demonstrate the worth of Lady Gregory, the much neglected but highly talented creative artist and person who has been overshadowed by W. B. Yeats. The book divides into seven chapters: approximately one-third of the work deals with Lady Gregory's place in the sociopolitical complex that formed the Irish Renaissance and its aftermath; the remainder attempts to assess the importance of her plays, her renderings of myth, and her other "minor" publications.

Chapter 1 locates the origins of several misconceptions concerning Lady Gregory's personality and works, investigates her childhood and her marriage to Sir William Gregory for influences upon her later writings, sketches her first "political" publications, and describes the basis of Lady Gregory's interest in the incipient revival in Ireland of the Gaelic language and ancient Irish customs. Chapter 2 discusses Lady Gregory's renderings of Irish folklore and mythology, emphasizing her *Cuchulain of Muirthemne* (1902), a prose account of the mythological Red Branch Knights, which first popularized outside of Ireland the deeds of the Celtic demigods. Discussion of this work and *Gods and Fighting Men* (1904) stresses Lady Gregory's depiction of the paramount role of women in the Irish sagas.

The third chapter of the book begins by defining the central role that Lady Gregory played in the beginning of the Irish Theatre movement, traces her defense of John Millington Synge's *The Playboy of the Western World* (1907)—citing especially her bravery in America when she opposed crowds hostile to the play —considers her specific influence upon Yeats's plays, and examines her heroic opposition to the censors of G. B. Shaw's *The Shewing-up of Blanco Posnet* (1909). Chapter 4 analyzes symbolism, organization, dialogue, and other aspects of Lady Gregory's *Seven Short Plays* (1909) and her *New Comedies* (1913). In order to provide starting points for future evaluations of Lady Gregory's dramatic works, this chapter combines a brief summary of each play with specific critical comments.

Chapter 5 discusses Lady Gregory's Folk-History plays (1912), showing how, in each of the three plays which make up the "first series" or "tragedies"—*Kincora, Grania,* and *Dervorgilla*—chaos is occasioned by a woman whose frustrated passion results in the destruction of her male counterpart. Discussion of the less stately, three "tragic comedies," the "second series," focusses on their variety of dramatic techniques and on their sometimes unsuccessful blending of seriousness and burlesque. The sixth chapter outlines the dire personal and political disappointments of Lady Gregory's last twenty years; examines the results of this psychic pain in Lady Gregory's splendid biography of her nephew, Hugh Lane; considers Lady Gregory's relationship with Sean O'Casey; and analyzes briefly a few of the plays of her last years. The final chapter of the book attempts to delineate, in a precise manner, the chief virtues and failings of Lady Gregory's career.

The study emphasizes above all the importance of Lady Gregory's dramatic contributions: the shorter plays, such as *The Rising of the Moon, Spreading the News, The Gaol Gate, The Workhouse Ward,* and *McDonough's Wife,* in which symbolism, characterization, and plot are so expertly blended that every line is essential to the overall work; the longer plays, such as *Grania* and *Kincora,* which clearly reveal Lady Gregory's profound understanding of the human motivations that underlie the public actions of historical figures; and the "comedies," such as *The White Cockade* and *The Image,* which deftly combine Lady Gregory's considerable wit with her intention in all of her endeavors: to add dignity to Ireland.

EDWARD A. KOPPER, JR.

Slippery Rock State College

Chronology

1906   Production of *Hyacinth Halvey, The Gaol Gate,* and *The Canavans.*

1907   January 26, first night of John Millington Synge's *The Playboy of the Western World:* the beginning of the riots. Production of *The Jackdaw* and *Dervorgilla.* Publication of *A Book of Saints and Wonders.*

1908   Departure of William and Frank Fay, the Irish actors, from the Abbey. Production of Lennox Robinson's *The Clancy Name* and with it the firm establishing of Realism in the theatre. Production of *The Workhouse Ward.*

1909   Publication of *Seven Short Plays;* presentation of G. B. Shaw's *The Shewing-up of Blanco Posnet* after Lady Gregory's refusal to submit to lord lieutenant's attempted censorship. Production of *The Image* and of the revised *Kincora.*

1910   First publication of *The Image* and of *The Kiltartan Wonder Book.* Miss Annie Horniman's decision to withdraw subsidy from the Abbey because of its failure to close on the day after Edward VII's death. Production of *The Travelling Man, The Full Moon,* and *Coats.*

1911   With Liebler and Co., theatrical managers, Lady Gregory escorts *The Playboy of the Western World* through United States amidst riots during winter of 1911–12. Production of *The Deliverer.*

1912   Publication of *Irish Folk-History Plays,* first and second series. Production of *McDonough's Wife, The Bogie Men,* and *Damer's Gold.*

1913   Publication of *New Comedies.* Hugh Lane resentfully makes a new will leaving his pictures to England; later drowns aboard *Lusitania,* and Codicil of Forgiveness is found. Publication of *Our Irish Theatre.*

1914   Production of *The Wrens.*

1915   Production of *Shanwalla.*

1916   Start of the Easter Rising. Publication of *The Golden Apple.*

1918   Production of *Hanrahan's Oath.*

1919   Publication of *The Kiltartan Poetry Book.* Production of *The Dragon.*

1920   Publication of *Visions and Beliefs in the West of Ireland.* Coming of the Black-and-Tans. Abbey temporarily closes. September 1920, Gort, the market town near Lady Gregory's girlhood home of Roxborough, almost burned to the ground by drunken soldiers.

1921   Lady Gregory lectures in Chelsea in effort to save the Abbey's finances. Publication of *Hugh Lane's Life and Achievement*. Lady Gregory's discovery of Sean O'Casey with *The Crimson in the Tri-colour*. Production of *Aristotle's Bellows*.

1922   Start of civil war in Ireland as Eamon de Valera, a Republican, refuses to join the Dail. Publication of *The Image and Other Plays*.

1923   Publication of *Three Wonder Plays*.

1924   Roxborough burned by an unaffiliated gang. Abbey becomes state-subsidized, a downward plunge. Production of *The Story Brought by Brigid*.

1926   Opening of O'Casey's *The Plough and the Stars*, the beginning of the demonstrations; O'Casey decides a few weeks later to leave Ireland. Publication of *A Case for the Return of Hugh Lane's Pictures to Dublin*.

1927   Loss of Lady Gregory's Coole estate to the forestry department. Production of *Dave*.

1928   Lady Gregory receives Sean O'Casey's "best play," *The Silver Tassie;* agrees with Yeats and Lennox Robinson, two Abbey directors, to reject the play. In 1929, O'Casey refuses to see her in London; his letters to her remain cordial from that point but never again deeply personal. Publication of *Three Last Plays*.

1930   Publication of *My First Play*.

1932   May 22, Lady Gregory dies rather than submit to another operation for cancer.

1947   Publication of Lady Gregory's *Journals*.

1974   Publication of Lady Gregory's autobiography, *Seventy Years*.

CHAPTER 1

The Sources of Inspiration

I   The Lady Gregory Myth

THE ample facts of Lady Gregory's life do not support the
unfortunate myths that surround her and that picture her as a
minor helper of William Butler Yeats, as an emotionally repressed
Victorian, and as a dramatist of little artistic integrity. Steps to
change this image and to reassess the considerable talents of the
Grand Lady of the Abbey have been undertaken by Miss Elizabeth
Coxhead in her excellent literary biography of Lady Gregory and by
Ann Saddlemyer and Hazard Adams in two brief but important
evaluations of Lady Gregory's works.[1] Lady Gregory is so many-
sided in the organizational powers that she revealed during the Irish
Theatre resurgence that much future critical attention should be
given to her. This critical-analytical but also biographical study
evaluates, among other items, Lady Gregory's adaptation of Gaelic
sagas and Kiltartan folklore, defines her role in the Irish Theatre
movement from its beginnings and through Lady Gregory's break
with Sean O'Casey in 1928, and discusses the merits, which have
been neglected, of her plays.

The Lady Gregory myths were formed in the tumultuous world of
Dublin politics before and shortly after the Easter Rising of 1916.
Lampoon was common in the era, and the most brutal personal
satire was usually answered in kind. Lady Gregory's satire, however, is carefully controlled by the artistic format of her plays; and
she rarely descends to invective. Then, too, Lady Gregory chose to
stay in Ireland through all the literary and political feuds while
several others adopted the policy of "to-hit-and-to-run" abroad.

Lady Gregory's false image was created primarily by James Joyce,
Oliver Gogarty (the Buck Mulligan of Joyce's *Ulysses*), and George
Moore. Most critics limit the Joyce–Lady Gregory relationship to
remarks made by Gogarty-Mulligan in the Scylla and Charybdis

15

episode of *Ulysses;* for Mulligan alludes to Joyce's derogatory review of Lady Gregory's *Poets and Dreamers* (1903), calls her an "old hake," and refers to Yeats's exorbitant praise of her *Cuchulain of Muirthemne* (1902): "The most beautiful book that has come out of our country in my time. One thinks of Homer."[2] Actually, Joyce's ridicule of Lady Gregory is scattered throughout *Finnegans Wake*, although the allusions were perceived by only a few members of the Joyce cult in the late 1920's and early 1930's. In the *Wake*, Lady Gregory is the primary source for Belinda the Hen who sits atop a prehistoric mound of earth to dig up the famous letter of *Finnegans Wake*, a product of Lady Gregory's folklore collecting. She is also the prototype of Kate the Sweep, and her duties performed as the "charwoman of the Abbey" are separated from any idealistic motives. Over one hundred allusions in the *Wake* relate to aspects of Lady Gregory's life and works.[3]

The sources of Joyce's intense dislike of Lady Gregory have yet to be uncovered, but they come in part from her membership in the ascendancy class and her oft-stated belief that she and Yeats had to work to add dignity to Ireland. Joyce, like many Dublin literary figures, was quite patriotic when it came to distrusting the landed gentry; and he was equally cosmopolitan in defending "art for art's sake." In addition, Lady Gregory's fidelity to her husband's memory—after his passing, she quirkishly wore black for forty years until her own death—was a contrast to Joyce's relationship with Nora Barnacle, his mistress, with whom he left for Zurich in 1904 but whom he did not marry until 1931.

Worst of all, however, Lady Gregory failed to recognize in the nineteen year old James Joyce the future genius of *Ulysses;* for she sent him to Paris with only five pounds. Oliver Gogarty provides some unusually reliable testimony about this material problem; and, in his description of Lady Gregory's dismissal of Joyce's previous attempt to secure funds, he speaks about a problem common to both men: "Who can measure how great was its [the Irish literary revival's] loss when Lady Gregory gave him the cold shoulder? Maybe her much-announced search for talent did not contemplate the talent latent in medical students' pals or wandering minstrels."[4]

Gogarty found Lady Gregory's humor boring. Moreover, he agreed with a group of critics who charged that Lady Gregory produced too many of her own plays; and he may have resented her antagonism to the budding Realists in the Irish Theatre, such as the predecessors of Sean O'Casey and the followers of John Millington Synge. Lady Gregory, of course, hated Synge's *The Playboy of the Western World* (1907) though she staunchly defended it. When Gogarty contemplated an evening at the Abbey Theatre, he suspected that the play ". . . would surely be something by Lady Gregory. I must get out before her namby-pamby humour deadens my spirits."[5] And again, "But the perpetual presentation of Lady Gregory's plays nearly ruined the Abbey. They were put on as curtain-raisers, comic reliefs, or they took the whole stage."[6] Since Lady Gregory admits in *Our Irish Theatre* (1913) that she began to write simply to provide comic relief from Yeats's heavy drama, Gogarty's appraisal is less than startling.

Of much greater importance is Gogarty's charge that Yeats wrote Lady Gregory's better plays. It is unfortunate that so flimsy an accusation should have been afforded any credence, for Gogarty's charge is based upon his ignorance of the type of collaboration in which the Abbey dramatists engaged. Although Una Ellis-Fermor clearly shows the essence of the "workshop" as she defines the nature of these playwrights' cooperation, Gogarty insists, "I almost got him [Yeats] to acknowledge his authorship of 'The Rising of the Moon [1907].' I think that he said that it was understood between himself and Lady Gregory that a play might be attributed to the one who had the idea!"[7]

Gogarty's suggestiveness is potent in creating a false image of Lady Gregory; but, with such circumstantial evidence, Gogarty is always Iago in his relationship with Lady Gregory, as when he asks, "How much of her plays did she write? Yeats had spent many months annually in collaboration with her in Coole Park, and I knew how generously Yeats presented me, for one, with golden lines or ideas."[8] As is later indicated, Yeats would have stepped completely out of character and style if he had created the popular successes of Lady Gregory.

Among other misrepresentations of Lady Gregory is that of George Moore who had met her in her youth and who had found her to be a "very earnest" young woman, who parted her hair in the middle and wore it flattened down on both sides. Moore once charged Lady Gregory with proselytizing and of using her influential position as a member of the landed gentry to entice her impoverished Irish peasants to give up their Catholicism. Although Moore withdrew this slur upon her character when he was

threatened with a lawsuit, his unfounded stress upon her supposedly militant Protestantism provided a major barrier between
her and the Irish Catholic populace of Dublin. When Moore
examined the coincidental organization of the Abbey troupe, he
indicated that, for a long time, the directors were Protestant; the
actors, Catholic. Moore describes Lady Gregory as a prude as well
as a close-minded Protestant, and this viewpoint persists in even
such a reputable critic as Herbert Howarth who remarks that "[t]he
elderly Sir William [Gregory] stood up to marriage with her for
twelve years. . . ."[9]

But Moore also attacked Lady Gregory's abilities in the most
sensitive area, her folklore collecting, which was made possible by
her power of communication with ordinary cottagers who lived near
her. In describing a visit to Lady Gregory's home at Coole Park to
discuss plans for *Diarmuid and Grania* (1901)—the play that resulted from a disastrous collaboration among Yeats, Moore, and
Lady Gregory—Moore reported that "Lady Gregory chattered on,
telling stories faintly farcical, amusing to those who knew the
neighbourhood, but rather wearisome for one who didn't. . . ."[10]
Moore may have been jealous of Lady Gregory's admiration for
Yeats; and he may have sensed that Lady Gregory disliked Moore so
intensely that he was not a welcome visitor at Coole. Lady Gregory
may have resented Moore's glib yoking of her attitudes with those of
her bigoted family at Roxborough, for she was a rebel from the
beginning.

Two figures who should have been sympathetic to Lady Gregory,
and who did try to be, failed to offset the negative image that Moore
and others had created of her. Sean O'Casey, while showing the
thoroughly human side of her frequently warm personality in *Inishfallen, Fare Thee Well* (1949), often projected his eccentricities
onto the subject. When he regards her too much with awe and
wonder, he consequently, almost unconsciously, destroys her sa-
cred image at every opportunity. His is the most famous picture of
Lady Gregory, the one that shows her as the female Samuel Johnson
and as the not quite successful blend of the restrained aristocratic
Protestant and the Irish Catholic commoner. He describes his first
meeting with her at the Abbey: "There she was before him." Like
one of her fairy folk, she had appeared from a dark corner of the
theater office when summoned by Lennox Robinson's "lean, wand-
like arm": "There she was, a sturdy, stout, little figure soberly clad

in solemn black. . . . A simple brooch shyly glistened under her throat, like a bejewelled lady making her first retreat. . . . Her face . . . hardy as that of a peasant, curiously lit with an odd dignity. . . . She looked like an old, elegant nun of a new order, a blend of the Lord Jesus Christ and of Puck. . . ."[11] In Casey's semi-autobiographical work, he is speaking, he believes, through the eyes of an impressionable youth. Other efforts by O'Casey to characterize Lady Gregory have done even more damage because he constantly refers to what he considered to be her poor taste in literature. In a well-known episode, he describes—despite his near blindness!—how he caught Lady Gregory reading J. Hartley Manners' comedy, *Peg o' My Heart* (1912), with rapt and loving attention while waiting for him at the Athenry railroad station. Then, too, all of Lady Gregory's dialogue in *Inishfallen* is recorded, needlessly, in her Western Ireland accent that so annoyed him: "Ah, dat book? I fordet who dave it to me. I just wanted to see what tort it was."[12] O'Casey was never fully a friend to Lady Gregory. He respected her as a son would a mother, he broke with her, he afterwards regretted the move, but he never understood her.

W. B. Yeats, another of Lady Gregory's friends, could have saved Lady Gregory's reputation by refuting the accusations made against her, especially those of Gogarty; but he chose not to do so; and, even worse, his tepid eulogy of Lady Gregory in *Dramatis Personae* (1936) damns her with faint praise. Yeats also ignores Lady Gregory's plays, the center of her contribution; and his omission is no less reprehensible when it is judged with the cold treatment that he meted out to his other colleagues during the last years of his life. Moreover, Yeats seems always to have dampened Lady Gregory's incentive; for, from the very beginning of the Irish Theatre, Yeats regarded her "first great service to the Irish intellectual movement" to be merely economic and organizational. She promised to raise the money necessary to form an Irish theater and dissuaded Yeats from building a theater in the suburbs of London. Writing in *The Trembling of the Veil* years later, Yeats remembers that, when Lady Gregory asked him what she could do to help the Irish movement, he replied "nothing." After that, he so discouraged her from writing her epic drama *Kincora* (1905) that she almost abandoned it but stayed with it and wrote a competent play.

From the start, Yeats did not trouble to discover that Lady Gregory had edited and written a few important political and social works before her first plays; and, during the golden days of her playwriting, he did not assess her worth as a creative artist in her own right. His few months of attendance by her side during her last illness were not sufficient compensation for his critical neglect; but, in all fairness, it must be admitted that Yeats's poetic gifts gave Lady Gregory her raison d'être. She was inspired to help Yeats add dignity to Ireland by constructing around him the Abbey Theatre, and she left in the process an excellent body of her own work.

Perhaps Yeats's greatest affront to Lady Gregory was unintended. He placed her in later life in the company of Queen Victoria in Phase Twenty-Four of *A Vision*, and Lady Gregory's true "mask" is self-reliance and organizational power.[13] Yeats saw the restraint in her personality, but he often ignored her spontaneity: "Lady Gregory, as I first knew her, was a plainly dressed woman of forty-five, without obvious good looks, except the charm that comes from strength, intelligence and kindness."[14] That she possessed "extreme vitality" Yeats discovered by hearsay from one who knew her at an earlier age.

Yeats so overshadowed Lady Gregory in the minds of most critics that anyone familiar with Lady Gregory's journey through America in the winter of 1911–12 with Synge's *The Playboy of the Western World* recoils from Sean O'Faoláin's comment about the play's production after 1921. He points out that it is now being acted without opposition, "largely through the tough courage of Yeats and the gallant support of his players."[15] Again, in discussing the censorship problems that the Abbey directors incurred in 1924 by accepting a state subsidy, he ignores the fact that Lady Gregory agreed to the grant only because Yeats would have closed the theatre without it. As O'Faoláin states, "It is to be remembered that the new Irish Government decided to subsidize the Abbey Theatre; which, at the time, seemed to us all a splendid gesture. . . ."[16]

II *Childhood and Marriage*

But the facts of Lady Gregory's life, its origins at Roxborough and her marriage at Coole, do correct the image damaged by some of her friends. Lady Gregory, Isabella Augusta Persse, was born March 15, 1852, at Roxborough in Galway. Her father, Dudley Persse, was twice married and had sixteen children, three by his first wife and thirteen by his second. Isabella Augusta—called Augusta throughout her childhood and even after her marriage—was lost in this large group of children since she was the twelfth child and the youngest girl. However, the family's interesting history and the many colorful figures who appear in it helped to form Lady Gregory's devotion to her Gaelic past, even though the Persses of Galway, Ireland, were a branch of the Percys of Northumberland, England. The staunch Protestant family, because of its Royalist affinities, acquired its extensive lands around Kiltartan and Kilchreest from two English kings with Catholic affections, Charles II and James II. Lady Gregory relates that George Washington also had been a friend of her grandfather, "who had been in America with his regiment." A case of stuffed birds at Roxborough was supposedly a gift from the general, and the Persse property enclosed a field named Mount Vernon.

At Roxborough, Augusta grew up in a world of rugged country life. The Persses depended upon their property for their livelihood; their estate was filled with the bustling activities of persons who were later to fill her plays; and the Persses' life was based upon a Puritan work ethic. According to Yeats, the family had originally settled in the center of Ireland; but, according to legend, it had found the visits of Lord Clanricard so expensive that it had moved away from the main road. The family purchased large tracts of Galway land that was beside the road from Gort (the market town nearest to Roxborough, which became the Cloon of Lady Gregory's comedies) to Loughrea. The Roxborough house was without literary pretensions, but a few ornamental books such as Thomas Moore's *Lalla Rookh* were scattered on the table, and once in a while a suitor would sing one of Moore's *Melodies* and play the piano. Although Augusta could not find works containing other than Moore's "faint sentiment," a stronger draught was attainable in the contraband Fenian pamphlets to which Augusta's Roman Catholic nurse, Mary Sheridan, introduced her. Yeats's estimate of Lady Gregory's youth is accurate: "The Persses had been soldiers, farmers, riders to hounds and, in the time of the Irish Parliament, politicians. . .";[17] but they had never been inclined toward developing esthetic interests.

Roxborough was situated in a wild area, and the natural setting was reflected in the behavior of some of Augusta's more interesting relatives. Looking at the record of her seven brothers, it is difficult to see evidence in her youth of what Gogarty has called her later "namby-pamby" humor. The brothers' feats of daring became legends in the area, probably because of the country folks' terror about their behavior. Yeats describes "how the wildest of the brothers, excluded by some misdemeanour from a Hunt Ball, had turned a hose on the guests; how, a famous shot, he had walked into a public-house in a time of disturbance and put a bullet through every number on the clock. . . ."[18] This independent spirit was supported by the self-sufficiency of the Persse family which never had to leave its property to acquire the goods necessary to its physical existence.

Although Lady Gregory shared her brothers' zest, her life can be read as a rebellion against both the despotism and the anti-intellectualism of the household. She did, however, possess a fond memory about her family's extreme self-reliance; and she reflected her family's courage when she braved the threat upon her life after Synge's *The Playboy of the Western World* had been brought to Chicago. In *Our Irish Theatre* (1913), written directly after her return to Ireland following the American tour, she recalls how Roxborough had once been attacked by Whiteboys, anti-British agrarian rebels active in the second half of the eighteenth century. Before *Our Irish Theatre*, she described in *Mr. Gregory's Letter-Box* (1898) an attack upon the property when her father, wishing to scare off the invaders, had aimed too truly at a tree that he had planned to use only to set his sights.

Sean O'Casey's re-creation of Lady Gregory's relationship to the stark natural surroundings of her childhood accords for the most part with her own estimate of their influence upon her youth. O'Casey finds that no Winnie the Pooh "gambolled in her garden; instead, her fancies were formed from the brown wind of Connacht, in summer soft and sensitive; in winter sending the foam flying frightened from the waves, beating the Galway coast, carrying the spindrift over the land to cover her window with its healthy, bitter brine."[19]

In a bedroom high up in the house, Augusta first heard the recital of Ireland's highly patriotic past from the lips of Mary Sheridan. Moreover, Lady Gregory views her interest in folklore not as a late discovery of something new but as a revival of instincts that had slept since her nursery days. The Irish Renaissance, as it was sponsored by Douglas Hyde and Yeats, stirred passions that had been instilled in her at Roxborough: "For a romantic love of country had awakened in me, perhaps through the wide beauty of my home, from whose hillsides I could see the mountain of Burren and Iar Connacht, and at sunset the silver western sea. . . ." Lady Gregory's most complete picture of this natural setting is found in her "An Emigrant's Notebook," an eleven thousand word unpublished manuscript, possibly written in 1884. Elizabeth Coxhead discusses at some length the significance of the piece both as a means of evaluating Augusta's attitudes toward Roxborough and as an example of her early powers of literary characterization.

The most significant figure at Roxborough was Catholic Mary Sheridan, the ardent Fenian, the reciter of ancient lore. Herbert Howarth points out that the hopes and sorrows of Ireland "filtered into sheltered homes through the servants. . . . The nurses had the greatest advantage."[21] Charles Stewart Parnell had his housekeeper at Avondale, and Lady Gregory had her moral and political compatriot in the woman who served the family for over forty years. The debt was not forgotten, for Lady Gregory states in her dedication to *Cuchulain of Muirthemne* that "I have told the whole story in plain and simple words, in the same way my old nurse Mary Sheridan used to be telling stories from the Irish long ago, and I a child at Roxborough."[22]

Mary's method of elucidating the heroic tales is an important source for Lady Gregory's own abilities to rearrange versions of a cycle. Lady Gregory's compilations of saga material are always a reasoned construction of Irish manuscripts salvaged from dusty Trinity College shelves; of already published accounts of the Fianna and the Red Branch Knights; and, most important, of the recordings from the uncertain memories of cottagers, for whom any cat or hare could be one of the Sidhe, the fairy descendants of the pagan Irish gods. One of the most delightful passages from the warmly personal beginning of *The Kiltartan Poetry Book* (1919) cites the instance of Augusta's trying to vex her governess by praising Malachi, who defeated the Danes in 1014, and his spoils of war, the collar of gold, "she no doubt as well as I believing the 'proud invader' it [the collar] was torn from to have been, like herself, an English one."[23]

Most significantly, Mary Sheridan aided the shy Augusta in her quiet but persistent rebellion against the dictatorial household which prohibited the teaching of Irish history. Mary filled Augusta with tales of Irish patriots like Hamilton Rowan (1751–1834), a friend of Wolfe Tone; and one of the nurse's lessons is recorded in Lady Gregory's play *The Rising of the Moon* (1907). Mary, who lived in the Rowans' household after Hamilton's pardon, was often subjected to his magnificent but unrestrained temper. Once she had come to the breakfast table with the children, "when suddenly Rowan flung away the newspaper he was reading, and seizing a knife dashed it at a picture of Lord Norbury, that hung on the wall, and slashed it across the face."[24] Norbury was known familiarly as either the punning or the hanging judge, but the role given him depended upon the speaker's situation. Again, Mary Sheridan recalled the landing of the French at Killala in Ireland in 1798 to assist in the United Irishmen Rebellion against the British, and the emotion generated by this tale surges through *The White Cockade* (1905).

In Lady Gregory's childhood, her rebelliousness appeared in brief trips to the stationer's shop where she bought green-covered Fenian booklets with the sixpence she had earned by faultlessly reciting her Bible lesson. She regarded the political split with her family as "the natural breaking of a younger child of the house from the conservatism of her elders."[25] Much of her spirit is seen in her editing *Ideals in Ireland* (1901), a collection of essays by leaders of the Irish Renaissance that range from polemics concerning the need to revive Gaelic to a methodical excoriation of England's faults. Writing in *Ideals in Ireland,* in December 1900, Lady Gregory defines civil disobedience in terms of Ireland's attempt to enlist the aid of the French in 1798. The idea for the candlestick emblem on the cover came from the granddaughter of a blacksmith: "She said he had made . . . many pikes for the rebels, but whenever the king's men were seen coming near the village, the pikes were hidden away, and he was found hammering at this candlestick: 'and that is the reason there are so many twists in it.' "[26]

Lady Gregory succeeded in turning the experience of her childhood into art when she had found her purpose in the Irish Renaissance. *The Bogie Men* (1912), a lightly satirical commentary upon man's slavish worship of images, as seen through the antics of two young chimney sweepers, has as its source an event that must have been painful, even though in the play only the joy remains. When Lady Gregory was writing the play, several Roxborough events flashed through her mind. First, a chimney sweeper had told Augusta that the only thing that had ever frightened him had not been the ghosts or Sidhe but the squealing and cries of two rats caught in a trap that had fallen down a staircase. She recalls in the same note the vision of the two lads who sometimes came to clean the chimneys and who walked five miles from Loughrea to do so: they were "little fellows with blue eyes shining out from soot-black faces, wearing little soot-coloured smocks."[27] The family physician had once visited a sick sweep and had found him "lying in a box, with soot up to his chin as bedding and blanket" (261). The same Olympian tolerance that makes Lady Gregory's world of Cloon truly comic may have led her to ignore sometimes the grosser abuses.

Another childhood experience, a vacation trip taken with her elders to Galway, is a basis for *The Rising of the Moon* (1907). The play concerns a police sergeant's change of heart when an unidentified man, presumably Hamilton Rowan, sings with him the old ballad of the play's title; and the sergeant then permits the minstrel to escape over the side of the dock. When Augusta had gone with her elders to fish for salmon in the river that courses past Galway Gaol, she "used to look with awe at the window where men were hung, and the dark, closed gate" (256–57). She often wondered if a man might escape by climbing down the wall and then, assisted by his friends, hide under a load of kelp in a fishing boat. The escape down the wall is worked into the burlesque known as *The Canavans* (1906). A more dour picture of the prison is given in *The Gaol Gate* (1906); in it, the dead hero's wife and his mother wait in vain for his release, not knowing that he has been hanged because he would not inform.

Finally, Roxborough, in its Irish name, Cregroostha, is the setting for Lady Gregory's hauntingly powerful adaption of Greek tragedy, *McDonough's Wife* (1912). The hero, who has no money to bury his wife, must rely upon his pipes to summon mourners. The mere piper, McDonough, by a subtle technique of expansion, becomes one with Orpheus; and he embodies in the play the magic powers that villagers had attributed to his father's tunes. Lady Gregory relates that, in her childhood, "there was every year at my old home . . . a great sheep-shearing that lasted . . . many days. On the last evening there was always a dance for the shearers and their helpers, and two pipers used to sit on chairs placed on a corn-bin to make music for the dance."[28] One of these men was invariably McDonough; he played to welcome Lady Gregory to Kiltartan following her marriage and to celebrate her son's coming of age. In this play, Lady Gregory succeeds almost as well as Synge in *Riders to the Sea* (1904) in casting a convincing halo of idealism over a common occupation.

Augusta's marriage to Sir William Gregory of Coole did not change her personality, but it certainly opened vast new areas in which her talents could find expression. Her life at Coole was a dream that had become reality, since the young woman had always yearned for the literary and the esthetic. And, by introducing her to the world of international politics, Sir William furbished the socially oriented interests of a woman who, as a girl, had started her own "business" to force local shopkeepers to lower their prices. Augusta probably saw in the widower a man who combined worldly sophistication with the ability to guide her into the society of men and women who were valued for their charm and not for their political dogmatism. From the first, she proved as a wife to be "quite a student."

The marriage took place on March 4, 1880, in Dublin with Augusta, twenty-eight, wearing gray, partially in mourning for a recently deceased brother, Richard, and partially because of the advanced age of the groom, sixty-three. The place of the marriage is significant, for Sir William preferred the life of the cities to that of Western Ireland. Lady Gregory was affected by his choice; and, after his death, she lived in London for a time with their friends, the Layards.

The disparity of age in the married Gregory couple has given rise to a good amount of speculation, but none is so interesting as the possible motives behind the match that Lady Gregory embodies in one of her best long plays, *Grania*, which she published in *Irish Folk-History Plays*, first series (1912), but which she would not allow to be produced, possibly because of its personal application. In this folk tragedy, Lady Gregory indicates that she knows her subject well; and she creates a slightly embarrassing but acutely psychological portrait of a woman who plans to marry the older Finn because of his kindness and because he is unlike the dark and wild King of Foreign. Yet Grania cherishes the warm emotional experience that came from her brief encounter years before with Diarmuid, with whom she now elopes on the eve of her marriage to Finn. Freudian criticism might see Diarmuid as the concrete image of the two suitors whom Lady Gregory's mother is said to have chased from the premises because of their unacceptable social position.

At any rate, Augusta's marriage seems to have been a happy one. Lady Gregory was able both to look beyond the public man and to locate her own individuality in the relationship. She wrote a pamphlet in defense of the nationalistic Egyptian, Arabi Bei, after Sir William thought it politic to drop the matter of Arabi's anticolonialist stands; she so delighted in the Grand Tour that dour Sir William wrote with surprise in his letter to Sir Henry Layard about her interest in Thothmes, Rameses, Knepf, and Shoofoo. Later in *Spreading the News* (1904), the first play of the Abbey Theatre, she uses her husband's teetotaling activities as governor of Ceylon for a satiric picture of the chief magistrate: "When I was in the Andaman Islands, my system never failed."[29]

Gregory's Coole was thoroughly interesting. The library was good enough to give plausibility to Lady Gregory's claim that Coole was the workshop of Ireland. It contained many volumes in Sanscrit, Greek, and Latin; and people at Coole combined appreciation of sophisticated books with graciousness toward wandering minstrels and tinkers. This dual tradition accounts for the blend of Romance and Realism in Lady Gregory's plays. As Joseph Hone states, "Many generations, and no uncultured generation, had left images of their service in the outlines of wood and fields at Coole, in sculpture and pictures, in furniture, in a fine library with editions of the classics and books on plants and agriculture."[30] It is no wonder that Coole became Lady Gregory's passion and that Yeats could find there a "life of order and of labour where all outward things were the signatures of an inward life."[31]

In general, Sir William's Coole residence and his travels with Lady Gregory to Ceylon, London, and Rome gave her a sense of permanence in the midst of change. In the battling between landlord and tenant during the late nineteenth century Land League Wars in Ireland, she retained a core of security that inspired her understanding sympathy, her "sense of feudal responsibility. . . ." " 'She has been', said an old man . . . 'like a servingmaid among us. . . .' a phrase of Aristotle's . . . motto: 'To think like a wise man, but to express oneself like the common people.' "[32]

III *Early Editing*

Lady Gregory's first published work, the five thousand word essay *Arabi and His Household* (1882), stems from the Gregorys' stay in Egypt during the winter of 1881–1882. Arabi Bey was an Egyptian officer who had advanced from the fellaheen class and who opposed the corruptions of the Egyptian hierarchy. Since this essay contains elements common to Lady Gregory's later style and point of view, it merits at least passing comment. It certainly reveals the beginnings of Lady Gregory's ability to penetrate artifice; for, from the outset, she was interested in the truth of a situation and took great pains to search for it.

For example, Arabi had been accused of torturing Circassian officers, the only indictable offense during the time of his virtually absolute rule of Egypt. Lady Gregory, searching the Blue-book laid before Parliament in proof of the accusation, could find only "a despatch [sic] from our Minister saying a European gentleman has told him that two natives had told him that they had heard cries proceeding from the prison where the Circassians were confined, from which is inferred that they were being tortured."[33] Moreover, the charge that Arabi expended funds on personal luxuries is refuted by Lady Gregory's description of a visit she made to his home with Lady Anne Blunt to call upon his wife. Here Lady Gregory demonstrates a precise knowledge of the market value of rugs and furnishings. The chief fault of the early work is the sentimentalized picture of Arabi himself: but in his heroism, Arabi is a prototype of the effective Sarsfield of *The White Cockade* (1905). Later, hearsay evidence and rash judgment become central to the plot of *Spreading the News* (1904), whose scenario was inspired by the story of a young girl who had "lost her name" because of a chance remark.

Lady Gregory's edition of her husband's autobiography was published in 1894; and her purpose in working with it was as humble as her motive for first writing plays when she decided to provide comic relief for Yeats's more important dramatic utterances. The autobiography, which had been written by Sir William between 1884 and 1891, had been intended for Sir William's son; and Lady Gregory published the manuscript to keep her husband's memory alive and to lend a hand to their Robert. Lady Gregory looked beyond the tired moralizing of the later pages to the eccentric but exciting scenes drawn from Sir William's early years. The dual ingredients of a captivating masculine personality and a restrained and pompously righteous middle age mark the book, and they helped to give Sir William's wife both rare subject matter and the distance to contemplate it. Of course, Lady Gregory omitted much embarrassing information from her edition of the *Autobiography*, just as she excised the naturalistic segments of the Irish sagas: "I have left out many passages that seemed too personal, or that might have vexed the living or slighted the memory of the dead."[34] Since she stresses her selectivity, what she includes affords some suggestions about her own personality.

Sir William's opening pages reveal the unsuccessful efforts of a reformed man-about-town to obliterate the enthusiasm for violence that had plagued his youth. Although his ancestors supposedly arrived with Cromwell and were called by such picturesque names as "Love is God Gregory," one was disinherited for cock fighting; and

Sir William's predecessors generally took part in tests of manhood, such as fighting duels, that were common in the earlier parts of the nineteenth century. For example, the autobiography describes the young subaltern whose plate of cauliflower was spoiled by a bullet as he sat at dinner; another youth won a duel by tricking his opponent into facing the sun; and Sir William himself lost favor with Lady Jersey by fighting one of the last duels on English soil without asking permission to use her grounds. Once, in Germany, he put to flight two street ruffians by boxing with closed fists, a method apparently not yet mastered in that country. But Sir William manages to glide like a spectre through most of the foibles of his time, even though his impregnability may be due to Lady Gregory's omission of damaging evidence.

Most important is the picture Gregory gives of the politicians of his day, and his portrait of Daniel O'Connell reveals some religious intolerance as well as the Irish propensity for building myths around their heroes. Once O'Connell exposed a plot to change a dead man's will by noticing the peculiarity of the expression that "[t]here was still life in him," which was offered as proof that the deceased was still alive when the alteration was made: it developed that a fly had been buzzing in the dead man's throat at that moment. Lady Gregory was later to record the testimony of one woman who credited O'Connell's spiritual intervention as the cause of her pregnancy; for, before O'Connell's prayers, she had been considered sterile.

Sir William, elected to Parliament in 1842, served until 1847, when he left political life for ten years; and, when he returned in 1857 as Knight of the Shire from Galway, he was a much sobered man. The famine of 1847 had changed his outlook, and the unhappy event contributed to the setting of Lady Gregory's *Dave* (1927). William Gregory's description of conditions during this potato blight is stark: "There was nothing . . . so horrible as the appearance of those who were suffering from starvation. The skin seemed drawn tight like a drum to the face, which became covered with small light-coloured hairs like a gooseberry."[35] Yet there creeps into the description in the autobiography a note of conservatism, and Sir William is impressed by the fact that peasants behaved with propriety during the ordeal. In acceptance of Establishment principles, he states that, although a few sheep were stolen elsewhere, crime was almost totally absent in his neighborhood. This lack of concern for human suffering is the beginning of a strain that characterizes the older man—a touch of the Henry Wilcox of E. M. Forster's *How-ards End* (1910). The Sir William that emerged from his experiences was a more stolid and less attractive sort than the dashing blade.

Lady Gregory ends her edition of the autobiography by including several letters from her late husband to Henry Layard, and the missives reveal Sir William's sometimes myopic vision. At one point, Lord Gregory tells Layard that he would trust some natives in his province as much as Englishmen, but that " '[w]eakness and moral and physical timidity are their main faults. . . .' "[36] And he concludes that only a firm hand can control their laziness. Significant are comments that Sir William makes about his wife—or the statements that Lady Gregory saw fit to include in the autobiography. William Gregory seems bothered by the legal arrangements needed for the wedding and complains of the lawyers' drawing up of the marriage settlements (February 15, 1880). From the beginning, he adopts a slightly condescending attitude toward his bride and approaches the Layards gingerly about their first meeting with Augusta. He feels constrained to ask his friends to receive his wife with the same enthusiasm that they prepare for a visit from him. In short, Sir William was to be pleasantly surprised about his wife: he soon realized that his bride was a finer asset than he had anticipated when Augusta opened her husband's eyes to the magic of a world that he had once enjoyed but had forgotten. Augusta thoroughly liked the prospect of nightingales, roses, boats on the Bosphorus, and photograph-taking through a tour of Holland that was meant to be primarily educational. He fared well in the marriage, for the union proved to be a rebirth for him.

Lady Gregory's first significant publication is *Mr. Gregory's Letter-Box* (1898), which shows a growing freedom in her attitude; and the independence maintained in Lady Gregory's marriage culminated after her husband's death in her judgments upon political leaders surrounding his grandfather, who was also a prominent British statesman. Her summarizing statement that they were honorable men is condescending, for the intent of the book is reinforced by a pun: they all looked at life with "kindly, if somewhat prejudiced eyes through party-coloured glasses."[37] In editing the correspondence of Sir William's grandfather, Lady Gregory stays aloof from any explicit condemnation of the intrigues and niceties of the era; but she selected details for highly effective, if subtle, satire.

Often administrative foibles are placed side by side with the dire consequences that they wrought upon the unfortunate—usually the Irish peasant. Whether portraying the Irish Catholic's hopes for emancipation or his desperate attempts to mold a leader after his aspirations, Lady Gregory carefully balances her work. Both style and subject matter appear later in the bantering peasants of Cloon and in the strain of mysticism present in Lady Gregory's works; but most significant to the critic of Lady Gregory's work are descriptions of early Victorian types who stumble through the pages of the letters, which incriminate the perpetrators by recording a naiveté supported by their belief that their way of doing things was not open to question. A man's career is ruined because his wife refuses to call upon the spouse of his superior, and a diplomat's son is suffocated in mud when thrown by his horse. Protocol demanded a constant tone in Ireland's version of Hampton Court, and rebellion was expressed only by destroying one's counterpart socially. In one letter, Gregory describes the tragic death of the young Duke of Dorset, whose horse fell on him; then he spends more time detailing a *contretemps* arising with Mrs. Arthur O'Connor, with whom Gregory refused to dine because her husband had tried to solicit help for the French.

Even more relevant as source material for Lady Gregory's plays, however, is the book's presentation of the underside of Irish life, the peasant and the police. The ominous presence of the Peelers, members of the Irish constabulary named after Sir Robert Peel (1788–1850), is found later in the atmosphere of *The Gaol Gate* (1906) and in the cool but misplaced assurance of investigating officers in *Shanwalla* (1915). The troubles of the 1820's foreshadowed the Black-and-Tan terrors a century later, and Lady Gregory states in the *Letter-Box*, "lonely indeed must be the road, deserted the railway station, where two dark figures with short capes and inadequate caps do not sooner or later appear, ostentatiously fingering their rifles and patrolling the Queen's highway."[38]

As familiar as Lady Gregory was with the twofold symbol of the occupation forces, the barrack and the jail, she unfortunately was thought to be in league with unthinking and oppressive segments of the ascendancy forces. She makes it clear in the *Letter-Box* that poverty is behind the crime in Ireland; and she at one point includes a reference to a study made by R. Willcocks, chief magistrate of Middle-third Barony, dated April 17, 1816: " 'The habitation is a small . . . filthy Cabbin, which very often contains a cow or a pig in the same appartment [*sic*] with some of the family. Their beds are in general straw, or the chaff of oats in a coarse bed-tick.' "[39]

IV *Influence of Gaelic*

The final early influence upon Lady Gregory's writing was the revival of the Gaelic language and the impetus which it gave to resurrecting ancient works. In her Kiltartan dialect, that rare throwback to the Tudor period, which is created by translating from Irish into English while keeping the syntax of the former, Lady Gregory fulfilled in her writings a key aim of the Celticists who sponsored the Irish Renaissance: a union of the mythological cycles. Standish James O'Grady, sometimes called the "Father of the Irish Literary Revival," stressed a return to the heroic tales. He wrote his famous "Bardic History," the *History of Ireland* (1878–1880); and Lady Gregory helped turn his turgid, ponderous prose into literature.

In her *Kiltartan Poetry Book* (1919), Lady Gregory explains her delay in studying Gaelic. As a child, inspired by Mary Sheridan, she had unsuccessfully sought permission to study with an old scripture reader who taught for a time in the parish of Killinane. A second opportunity vanished as Standish H. O'Grady, author of *Silva Gadelica* (1892), was banished from the house by Augusta's mother when he took an interest in Augusta's sister. At that time, Lady Gregory was prepared to devote full time to becoming a true Gaelic scholar. During her marriage, Lady Gregory worked with a Gaelic grammar and with a gardener who lost interest in the project when he felt that the mistress was patronizing him.

Finally, after her husband's death, her son Robert, having won the classical entrance examination at Harrow, decided to master Gaelic; and he asked Edward Martyn, the neighbor at Tillyra, for a tutor. Martyn sent back an old Irish Bible, and mother and son began to labor over it. The task was facilitated by Father O'Growney's grammar and by the inspiration of Douglas Hyde's establishment of the Gaelic League in 1893, for "through it country people were gathered together in the Irish speaking places to give the songs and poems, old and new, kept in their memory. This discovery, this disclosure of the folk learning . . . was the small beginning of a weighty change. . . . The imagination of Ireland had found a new homing place."[40]

According to Lady Gregory, the death in 1891 of Charles Stewart
Parnell, the powerful and controversial political leader, combined
with the Gaelic revival, unleashed the imagination of Ireland and
effected a "moment of a new impulse in literature. . . ." The revival
appealed to Lady Gregory's own fancies; she needed to search no
longer in arcane social events for inspiration, for a world to explore
was brought to her doorstep: "among farmers and potato diggers and
old men in workhouses and beggars at my own door. . . ."[41] Lady
Gregory found that Douglas Hyde's *Love Songs of Connacht* (1893),
in its concreteness and fidelity to the elemental passions, formed a
welcome contrast to the pale lyrics of Thomas Moore; and Yeats's
mystical or "Celtic" view of the imaginative Sligo country folk added
a new depth to Lady Gregory's perception of her surroundings.

As part of her activities, Lady Gregory had a headstone made for
the semilegendary nineteenth century poet Raftery; and, in the
house of a stonecutter, she found a manuscript of his poems. She
also listened to a hundred year old man who told her of Cuchulain's
slaying his son by accident and to a basketmaker who voiced the
common, derogatory opinion of the country people concerning
Grania, the lover of Diarmuid, who married Finn after the king had
slain Diarmuid: Finn was a wise man, but he wasn't smart enough to
check Grania. Lady Gregory found in the legends preserved by
these cottagers a refreshing contrast to the Jansenistic Catholicism
that had replaced the old myths. Though religion offers ample re-
wards in the afterlife, to Lady Gregory it "has left Heaven itself far
off. . . . I think it is perhaps because of this that the country poets of
to-day and yesterday have put their dream . . . into exaggerated
praise of places dear to them."[42]

Lady Gregory's advocacy of the ancient Gaelic sagas placed her in
opposition to the Irish (and English) Establishment; and, in her note
to *Ideals in Ireland* (1901), she speaks of the butcher, who is one of
three individuals in a community; the other two are the baker and
the candlestick maker. She recognizes the hem of the butcher's blue
apron under the frock coat of a commissioner of education who is
engaged in cutting through the veins that unite the present with the
past. Part of this attitude, Lady Gregory feels, is also seen in the
"Chinese Wall," the iron fence by which Trinity College separates
itself from Ireland.

CHAPTER 2

Folklore and Mythology

I *The Celtic Revival*

A number of forces sparked the revival of folklore interest during the 1890's in Ireland. As part of a new Romanticism, the Celtic cult can be regarded as a natural result of the stress of Jean-Jacques Rousseau and John Ruskin upon the peasant and the remote past. Then, too, the revival was stimulated by the recent discoveries of mythic patterns in other countries that were synthesized in Sir James Frazer's *The Golden Bough* (1890). In Ireland, the revival "possessed a strong tendency toward melancholy";[1] but the sense of *place* was so strong that it prevented exorbitant vagueness. Above all, however, the Celtic resurrection was viewed by those who sponsored it as a return to an ancient idealism.

Yeats and Lady Gregory recognized the vitality in legends that could survive in ever self-aggrandizing forms from the Old Irish civilizations. Joyce in *A Portrait of the Artist as a Young Man* (1916) describes Ireland's coming toward the light. For "A. E.", George Russell, the process was mystical; for Joyce, cosmopolitan. Lady Gregory, influenced by Yeats's *Celtic Twilight* (1893), which resuscitated in her the folklore embers originally lighted by Mary Sheridan, argues that speakers of the West Irish ballads should soon find a leader to express in prophetic tones the emotions of his people. She illustrates with the Hebrews of the Old Testament: "the sorrow of exile was put into the hundred and thirty-seventh Psalm, and the sorrow of death into the lament for Saul and Jonathan, and the yearning of love into what was once known as 'the ballad of ballads,' the Song of Solomon."[2] The West Irish ballads reveal, to her, a people verging on a great discovery.

Faith in the Irish peasant's heritage was fortified by the belief current among the Celticists—though Lady Gregory hated the word—that the heroic sagas were examples of Joy and Light and that they lacked the somber and oppressive foreboding of the Greek and Roman classics. In the Gaelic cycles, men supposedly faced their enemies happily and met death merrily. Whatever be the merits of this position, which seems indefensible without considerable editing of the saga texts, this view forms the basis for Yeats's appreciation of Lady Gregory's *Gods and Fighting Men* (1904). In his preface, Yeats sees the Celtic Romance as a mystery springing not from the darkness of the Gothic nations "but out of great spaces and windy light."[3] One wonders how Yeats was able to ignore the death of Cuchulain's son in his comment, the relentless search of the small-minded Finn for Diarmuid, and the wasted energy of the warriors in the cycles who argue over trivia.

A stronger basis for the popularity of the folklore revival may be the sentimental view of the peasant promulgated by Douglas Hyde when he pictures the cottager as sorrowful, bruised, and worn down in his own land but as able to find an almost magical buoyancy in "excessive foolish mirth, or in keening and lamentation."[4] Since Hyde's view was too close to that of the stage Irishman who is never far from a smile or a tear, Lady Gregory spent much of her time trying to erase such an image; and, when she appears impersonal, she is often attempting to strike a balance between bathos and the excessive reforms of the Nationalists. However, Ivor Brown, who contrasts the supposed Realism of G. B. Shaw with the allegedly sterile fantasy of Lady Gregory, believes that Shaw avoided entanglement in the early Irish Literary Theatre "with its tendency to harp . . . on the old legends of Cuchulain and the often-sung sorrows of Deirdre. . . ."[5] Shaw, Brown indicates, had seen the Dublin slums; but Lady Gregory "liked questioning the old women round Coole about the faeries, apparently a numerous tribe, whom they saw in the woods."[6] Such a view of Lady Gregory's folklore collecting ignores the massive excavations of the Irish Revivalists and their very different points of view toward their findings.

The prophetic content of Irish literature is best examined by looking into its long tradition. The theme of the deliverer had been in constant usage for nine centuries when Yeats, George Moore, Lady Gregory, "A. E.", and Joyce picked up the thread. The literature of the seventeenth and eighteenth centuries contains much mourning over the "passing of the old order" and many denunciations "of the evils perpetrated by the foreigner. . . ."[7] A somber tone is seen in a poem by Fearflatha O'Gnive composed shortly after

1612 which expresses doubt that the long awaited deliverer would come. In the sixteenth century, Hugh O'Neill, champion of Irish hopes against the determined "invaders," the English, was regarded as the savior prophesied by St. Columbkill. In Lady Gregory's short play *The Deliverer* (1911), she uses the popular variation of the messianic theme, the return of the hero, whether he be Finn Mac-Cool or Parnell. Throughout Joyce's *Ulysses* (1922), allusions are made to the possibility that Parnell was not really buried but that his coffin was filled with stones; and Yeats believed in his vision of a battle to be fought in "The Valley of the Black Pig" in which the messiah would conquer Ireland's enemies in a great conflagration.

Ironically, folklore collecting and collating received great impetus from the attempts of Trinity College to ignore the Gaelic past. When Trinity, in response to an investigation begun in 1900 by a commission established to correct secondary education in Ireland, condemned both saga and folklore, Yeats, Lady Gregory, and many other writers who were otherwise incompatible united to refute a common foe. For Lady Gregory, the blow delivered by Trinity College was great. She had been awakened by the writings of Hyde and Yeats, and the Gaelic League was now under assault. But she knew that Yeats was the person to see if one wished to volunteer one's services.

Although Yeats expressed great surprise that Lady Gregory had the ability to create, he decided to give her a chance. In a previous meeting, he had told her of Alfred Nutt's offer to supply him with translations of the heroic cycles if he would select the choice parts and style them in an attempt to do "what [Thomas] Malory had done for the old French narratives."[8] The comparison with Thomas Malory is significant since it probably helps to account for Yeats's claim that Lady Gregory became the Malory of Ireland with her *Cuchulain of Muirthemne* (1902). In any case, Lady Gregory had asked Yeats a few days later for permission to attempt the project; and she had also offered to provide her own translations and to find others. She had been angered by the "eminent Trinity College professor"[9] who described the sagas as silly and indecent, and a week or two later she took to Yeats an heroic tale that she had translated into the Kiltartan dialect of her neighborhood.[10]

Lady Gregory was proud of her corner of the folklore market; and when, on a trip to the Aran Islands, she spotted Synge among the visitors, she was as angry about his presence as he was about hers.

She certainly attained a competence in her work that was acknowledged very soon by Synge, and she repeats with justifiable pride Synge's comment to Yeats after the publication of her *Cuchulain of Muirthemne* that in the work he had found the dialogue he had been trying to master. To Lady Gregory he wrote, " 'Your *Cuchulain* is a part of my daily bread.' "[11] Later he felt that Lady Gregory's *The White Cockade* (1905) "had made the writing of historical drama again possible."[12] She believed in the sincerity of Synge's judgment about even her earlier *Cuchulain*, and she alludes to it in *Our Irish Theatre* (1913) and in her Introduction to the *Kiltartan Poetry Book* (1919).

She was influenced in her own collections of folklore by two slim volumes published in 1893: Douglas Hyde's *Love Songs of Connacht* and W. B. Yeats's *The Celtic Twilight*. Lady Gregory was impressed by Hyde's writings long before she met him in the summer of 1898.[13] Indeed, it was not difficult to like "Duggie," for his manner was as spontaneous and as sincere as his work. His tumbling thoughts, Yeats felt, proceeded from unbounded joy; and his choice of words avoids preciousness. Lady Gregory cites Hyde's influence: "It was only a few years ago, when Douglas Hyde published his literal translations of Connacht Love Songs, that I realized that, while I had thought poetry was all but dead in Ireland, the people about me had been keeping up the lyrical tradition that existed in Ireland before Chaucer lived. While I had been looking in the columns of Nationalist newspapers for some word of poetic promise, they had been singing songs of love and sorrow in the language that had been pushed nearer and nearer to the western seaboard."[14]

Lady Gregory had done quite a bit of research, and, using the psychological tools that she had learned, she worked in the cottages. Moreover, she soon discovered that a bit of tobacco and a spot of whisky loosened the tongues of the oldsters. Also, she may have found helpful Hyde's instructions to folklore collectors in his *Beside the Fire* (1890). Lady Gregory was influenced, in addition, by Hyde's technique of informally gathering information from the cottagers. She mentions that she chose to transcribe legends in the speech used in the thatched houses "where I have heard and gathered them. *An Craoibhin* [Hyde's Gaelic name] had already used this Gaelic construction, these Elizabethan phrases, in translating the *Love Songs of Connacht*, as I have used it even in my creative work."[15] Sincerely grateful to Hyde, she recalled her debt to him in the midst of the severe sorrow occasioned by the death in combat of her son, Robert, during World War I.

One of Hyde's most influential tales was that composed by Tumaus Loidher (Strong Thomas) Cosdello, or Coisdealbhach (foot-shaped) for Una MacDermott. Cosdello, who had lived in the time of Charles II, had owned quite a bit of land which he lost through Cromwell's coming—the reverse of the Persses' fortunes. Tumaus provided one source for Lady Gregory's characterization of Grania, who eloped with Diarmuid in the midst of the preparations for her marriage with the considerably older Finn. Old MacDermott chose the prospective husband of his daughter, Una; and he once told Una after a dinner to drink the health of the person whom she liked best in the assembly. When she toasted Tumaus, her father slapped her across the head. And Tumaus's song, "Fair Una," helps to support Lady Gregory's belief that romantic love is not a motivating factor in the Irish male. Its line, "I would rather than two sheep if I had Una"[16] ("a lamb," a play upon the word), is typical of the concern for things other than love in this "love poem."

Finally, allusions to religion in *Love Songs of Connacht* are quite curious but essential to an understanding of the peasant as presented by Hyde, Yeats, and Lady Gregory. Hyde's cottagers are often defined by their feelings towards Christian dogma, and they never deny a single doctrine. Catholicism is as self-evident to them as their own existence, and they question only the way in which the church's teachings can be applied to a situation. As for Yeats's influence upon Lady Gregory's view of the peasant, *The Celtic Twilight* is most powerful when Yeats describes objectively and without conclusions the doings of the rugged cottagers, who, he feels, illustrate the "striving after a something never to be completely expressed in word or deed."[17] They manifest the Celtic melancholy and in the core of their being long for "infinite things the world has never seen."[18]

But the story of one strong farmer supports Yeats's other view that the Irish peasant is possessed of a Chaucerian love of life, and the narrative probably influenced Lady Gregory's *The Workhouse Ward* (1908), which is her picture of a divided Ireland that is symbolized in two quarrelsome old men. Yeats's "knight of the sheep" lived to the north of Ben Bulben and Cope's Mountain and was plagued by the tax collector, O'Donnell. His daughter was kind to O'Donnell by insisting that her father offer him whisky in the kitchen of their home, for the tax gatherer had recently lost his son. The two men got along for a few hours, and the farmer offered to show his new friend the way home. Half way to the main road they came across one of the farmer's hired hands who was working late, ploughing the land to earn income that would soon go to the tax collector. The farmer was reminded of the function of his visitor, and began to swear at him again.

II *Peasant Lore*

Poets and Dreamers (1903) is Lady Gregory's compilation of several types of anecdotes related by the cottagers whom she visited while collecting folklore. It illustrates many aspects of the Irish peasant personality. The opening forty-five pages concerning Raftery blaze with the cottagers' devotion to locale and to their local poet; a later section, "Workhouse Dreams," records the childlike fantasies and fairy tale dreams of the old men and of the physically incapacitated young men in the Gort Workhouse. Another section tells of Biddy Early, the gay and often helpful witch, whose list of herbs makes her a prime apothecary. The book ends with a translation from the Gaelic of four plays by Douglas Hyde, one of which is *The Twisting of the Rope.*

Poets and Dreamers is valuable for the brilliance of a few of its episodes; for its ability to lay bare the peasant mind, the products of which are found in the livelier parts of Yeats's early plays composed with Lady Gregory's help; and for its use as source material for many of Lady Gregory's dramas, such as *The Travelling Man* (1910), *Damer's Gold* (1912), and *Hanrahan's Oath* (1918). *Poets and Dreamers* underplays the mystical side of the cottager that was stressed in Yeats's *The Celtic Twilight,* although Lady Gregory's rhetoric and language have at times characteristics of Yeats's didacticism. Fortunately, she describes the "visionary" intuitions of the peasants mainly in the "Workhouse Dreams" section of *Poets and Dreamers;* and the remainder of the book is realistically humorous and uncontaminated by spurious spirituality.

Lady Gregory's frequent objectivity in *Poets and Dreamers* is evidenced in her opening comments concerning two old women, who, in the "Raftery" section, argue the merits of Raftery and the rival poet, Callinan. The discussion is heated because so great is the power of poets in Ireland that the people once cut out the tongue of O'Higinn after he had satirized them. But even O'Higinn's power does not equal Raftery's, avers one "bedridden" old woman, who joins the other two and suddenly begins to sing Raftery's "Bridget Vesach" "as long as her breath lasted. . . ."[19] Lady Gregory is also objective because, though she readily sees the merits of the remarkable Raftery, she is all the more studious in finding the weak points in his work. Thus she adds plausibility to her account; in so doing, she enunciates an early esthetic for her own writing. Raftery has much more realism and power that Callinan, Lady Gregory believes, but he too frequently falls prey to stock diction and vapidity. Such are his allusions to Helen and Venus, which partake of "formula" poetry; then too his diction is often wildly exaggerated. But he can certainly turn a striking phrase, Lady Gregory admits, in his lines on death and judgment: he sees that the cheeks of the dead are " 'cold as the snow that is at the back of the sun.' "[20]

The "Raftery" section relates that the farmers are afraid of the poet and dare not refuse him a ride when he stands by the side of the road. Lady Gregory explains that his poetic strength was phenomenal, for he once wrote a love song to Mary Hynes that caused her to die young. On another occasion he withered a bush by his curse. This gesture and other detrimental activity by poets caused them to be banished in the time of St. Columbkill: " 'Sure no one could stand the satire of them.' "[21] But with all his power, Lady Gregory explains, Raftery is a beggar. He travels about until he "marks" a house; he then goes inside, and he usually is thronged by the neighboring populace. Once, though, he lost a match of wits to Callinan, who made him weep. A maid servant reports that Callinan alluded to Raftery's impoverished upbringing and thus wounded his pride.

In "Herb-Healing" (also a part of *Poets and Dreamers*), Lady Gregory describes Bridget Ruane, or Biddy Early, who was named after a famous witch doctor. Biddy was respectable looking, Lady Gregory was told, and she wore the red petticoat and blue cloak of the country folk. Lady Gregory was able to learn of her activities because she had already a store of arcane knowledge in herbs and potions so great that it startled the farmers who spoke with her about magic. A man from East Galway wondered how Lady Gregory had heard of Garblus, the herb " 'for things that have to do with the faeries.' "[22] This type of knowledge is shared by members of "The

Wandering Tribe," who resemble hobbits in their lack of consideration for a host.

In its plausible use of fantasy, the section of *Poets and Dreamers*
entitled "Workhouse Dreams" anticipates Lady Gregory's two later
works: *The Kiltartan Wonder Book* (1910) and *A Book of Saints and
Wonders* (1907). The extensive chapter effectively utilizes the
dramatic framework in which the workhouse inmates tell their
stories. The men emerge as realistic figures enclosed by a precise
physical setting: "We [Lady Gregory and the men] sat in a gravelled
yard, where only the leaves of a few young sycamores told that
spring had come. Some of the old men sat on a bench against the
whitewashed wall of a shed, in their rough frieze clothes and round
grey caps, and others stood round, pressing closer and closer as
their interest in the story grew."[23] The fantasy tales form an excellent contrast to the barren housing in which they are recited. Lady
Gregory blinks at the implied surroundings—though Gort Workhouse was no chamber of horrors—and cites an old proverb: " 'It is
from a deep narrow well the stars can be seen at noonday.' "[24]

The stories in "Workhouse Dreams" contain all the tricks common to the Irish fairy tales: talking heads; food and drink that come
from unlikely places like a bull's horn; the ubiquitous slumber pin,
which can put one who is touched by it instantly to sleep; and the
device of the recurrent number. Three is a favorite, and at one point
the three daughters of the king of Spain are helped by three giants.
In another tale, one youth performs Herculean tasks with the help
of the Sidhe to win his girl. The jester, however, is more in keeping
with historical tradition since he can win all by his wit. He is an
important figure who reappears in the Irish sagas and who possesses, in Lady Gregory's opinion, the mercurial wit of G. B. Shaw.

III *Cuchulain and Finn*

Lady Gregory's *Cuchulain of Muirthemne* (1902) is, in many
ways, a massive contribution to the Irish Renaissance. Despite its
occasional lapses into an ineffectual Kiltartan and its sometimes too
lengthy digressions, it comes close to unifying the vast body of
materials that make up the tales of Ireland's mythological Red
Branch warriors. Moreover, *Cuchulain* first made the Irish sagas
popular outside of Ireland; for, though Standish James O'Grady had
revived such sagas within the country, Lady Gregory's *Cuchulain*
first introduced them to America. There President Theodore

Roosevelt was a most avid fan; and, in his defense of Lady Gregory during the riots over Synge's *The Playboy of the Western World,* he recalled his debt to her book.

Lady Gregory's *Cuchulain* is a lengthy prose narrative that concerns the deeds of the Red Branch Knights, whose king was Conchubar (or Connor) and whose greatest warrior was Cuchulain. In her account, she draws upon the work of many predecessors—such as Standish O'Grady, George Sigerson, and Samuel Ferguson—who had published their major translations of the Red Branch saga during the 1880's. By adding individuating touches and by popularizing the legends surrounding Cuchulain, Lady Gregory, along with the other writers in the Irish Renaissance, helped to make him the rallying point of the Easter Rising of 1916.[25] Cuchulain's futile struggles against superior forces represented for the rebels of the Easter Rising tiny Ireland's losing battle against English imperialism. Then too, Cuchulain's sad career blended with the melancholy strain that was part of the Celtic revival. Yeats, in his play *On Baile's Strand* (1903), describes the powerful emotions of Cuchulain after he unknowingly killed his own son: Cuchulain expresses and mitigates his anger when he is told what he has done by striking with his sword at the relentless waves.

Although Lady Gregory's complaint that Trinity College's neglect of things Irish left the task of compiling the epics to a "woman of the house,"[26] her goal in writing *Cuchulain* was a positive one. Her purpose in all the saga work was dual: artistic and patriotic. She dedicated her edition of *Cuchulain* to the people of Kiltartan; and she informed them that, though they had readily at hand the legends of Finn and Goll and Oisin in the memories of the old people, little about Cuchulain could be found.

Lady Gregory opens *Cuchulain of Muirthemne* with a description of Conchubar, the uncle of Cuchulain: Conchubar was king of Ulster, the geographical center of the work, and he held his court in Emain Macha. To Conchubar's court came the stripling Cuchulain, who is seen as a boy at the beginning of the book and who is still a youth at its end. Leaving his foster parents—an epic convention—he set out with his hurling stick, his little dart, and his spear. Then he was called only Culain, and he won his way with the children playing at war in Conchubar's court. Shortly after, he became known as Cuchulain, the hound of Culain, by killing a vicious dog that attacked him. Cuchulain was early destined, like Achilles, to a short and famous existence but, unlike the Greek semigod, who had the help of his mother Thetis, Cuchulain won his own dubious fate by his Irish wit. He volunteered for battle before his time after overhearing the words of Cathbad the Druid, which were not meant for his ears. His quick mind and his bloodthirsty spirit made his first venture in battle successful.

Cuchulain's downfall begins when he is forced to kill in single combat his fellow student of the past, Ferdiad. Here Lady Gregory's imaginative powers in reconstructing the old versions prove limited, for the supposed deep and abiding friendship between the two men was never developed in *Cuchulain*. Many of the errors in *Cuchulain of Muirthemne* are minimized, however, by Lady Gregory's compelling narrative of Cuchulain's last days. Most influential in the Irish Renaissance is the hero's killing of his son, Conlaoch, through ignorance of his identity. Not wanting to kill Cuchulain, the lad threw his spear weakly and to the side; Cuchulain, for once betrayed by his "hero light," aimed true and slew the boy. Only the spell of Cathbad the Druid, who appears here, at the end of the book, as he did at the beginning of Cuchulain's warrior career, prevented the remorseful hero from taking his life. Lady Gregory's description of Cuchulain's death is lyrical. The hero sees his fate clearly and knows that he will die in the upcoming war for Ulster's survival. The Morrigu herself, the crow of battle, is saddened when Cuchulain expires and when the Grey, Cuchulain's horse, kills many opponents to avenge his master's death before he himself is destroyed.

Several elements of Cuchulain's characterization in the Irish sagas pose problems for modern interpreters; and the most difficult is his "distortion"—the flight-or-fight reaction that Cuchulain undergoes in times of great stress. The old manuscripts give a detailed picture of Cuchulain's grotesque physical change to account for his sudden bursts of strength. Lady Gregory simplifies the metamorphosis by calling it the "hero light" and by objectively describing the deeds performed under its influence, such as Cuchulain's leaping over walls and hills.

One other "movement" in the Red Branch cycle of Irish mythology that Lady Gregory records with great effectiveness in *Cuchulain of Muirthemne* is the complex of events leading to the suicide of Deirdre, the Irish Helen of Troy who broke her vow to marry Conchubar and eloped to Scotland with her love Naoise and his two brothers. Deirdre's history elicits some of Lady Gregory's finest writing despite the fact that Lady Gregory liked Deirdre less than Grania since she preferred Grania's choice of a difficult life (marriage with Finn after Diarmuid is dead) to Deirdre's chosen suicide. Moreover, Lady Gregory's qualified point of view, her dislike of Deirdre's "solution" to her problems, gave her excellent control of the narrative in *Cuchulain*, permitting her an objectivity that would have been impossible for an author who identified totally with her heroine.

As Deirdre's tale opens, the joyous occasion of her birth is marred by the prediction that she will some day cause much pain and suffering as her name in Gaelic indicates since it means "of the sorrows." Because of the prediction, Deirdre was reared away from civilization but was found by Conchubar, who prepared her from girlhood to be his bride. He had a nurse instruct her in the ways of love; and Lady Gregory suggests that, after the course, Deirdre blushed whenever she heard the word "love."

One of Lady Gregory's contributions to the Deirdre legend lies in her version of how the flight of the lovers, Deirdre and Naoise, ends because of the misty designs of Fergus, who comes to them as a messenger from Conchubar who is ostensibly offering amnesty. When Fergus tempts Naoise to return to the tribe by appealing to his nostalgia, he reinforces Lady Gregory's view that the Irishman will choose country over romantic love. Thus Lady Gregory's Fergus differs considerably from the Fergus of Yeats's poetry. In Lady Gregory's portrayal, he is the slightly sinister but generally naive messenger; and he is a stalwart supporter of Conchubar. In Yeats's famous poem, "Who Goes with Fergus," he is the idealistic king who surrendered his throne to Conchubar in order to wander in the woods to compose poetry and to commune with spirits.

Yeats finds the language used in Lady Gregory's *Cuchulain* to be less important than the work's elegance and Celtic spirit. Unadvisedly lumping together both her *Cuchulain* and her inferior *Gods and Fighting Men* (1904), he regards them as made possible by Lady Gregory's semifeudal past at Roxborough: "her inherited sense of caste, her knowledge of that top of the world where men and women are valued for their manhood and their charm."[27] He also views *Cuchulain* as a product of Lady Gregory's readings in Bishop Thomas Percy's *Reliques of Ancient English Poetry* (1765), in the Scottish ballads, and in Thomas Malory; for Yeats attributes to these early works the fact that Lady Gregory found her dialect to be a perfect medium of expression. He definitely agrees with those who find it meritorious for Lady Gregory's ancient kings to speak in Kiltartan, which language, Yeats feels, is a mirror of Lady Gregory's true Western Ireland self.

Cornelius Weygandt's early analysis of Lady Gregory's work in myth in his *Irish Plays and Playwrights* (1913) finds that Lady Gregory added her "personality" to the earlier works of O'Curry, Stokes, and O'Grady, even though she does not tell the tales "just as they are."[28] He believes that her translations are "interpretative and artistic" as opposed to their "literal" work.[29] One difficulty, however, is found in the Kiltartan which, Weygandt feels, is suited to the cottage nature of the Finn cycle but is less appropriate to the court romance of Cuchulain. However, Weygandt comments that the language adds the needed foreign flavor "that we intuitively feel the need of in a translation."[30]

A current estimate of Lady Gregory's *Cuchulain of Muirthemne* is offered by Thomas Kinsella, the brilliant translator of the *Táin Bó Cuailnge*, the prose epic that forms the center of the Ulster cycle. Kinsella treats Lady Gregory's work with respect: after searching through many translations of the deeds of the Red Branch Knights, Kinsella relates that he "emerged with the conviction that Lady Gregory's 'Cuchulain of Muirthemne', though only a paraphrase, gave the best idea of the Ulster stories."[31] According to Kinsella, however, Lady Gregory did err in "some important ways," by "refining away the coarse elements and rationalising the monstrous or gigantesque. . . ." To Kinsella, "[a] strong element in the sagas is their directness in bodily matters: the easy references to seduction, copulation, urination, the picking of vermin, the suggestion of incest in 'How Cuchulain was begotten,' and so on. This coarseness was a source of some uneasiness to Lady Gregory . . . but it seems very mild to a modern reader. . . ."[32] Finally, Kinsella complains that the *Táin Bó Cuailnge* is "inadequately represented" in Lady Gregory's work, a lacuna which occasioned his own translation.

Lady Gregory, knowing Gaelic, whereas O'Grady was weak in the language, keeps closer to the original text (except where sex and violence are concerned), arranges the episodes to better advantage, and "invents" the original style that she was later to use in her plays. Although much of the same material contained in Lady Gregory's work had been gathered by Eleanor Hull and Whitley Stokes, her writing brings "that last creative touch needed to transfuse the various materials into one homogeneous body."[33] With her desire to examine all versions of an event, moreover, Lady Gregory's additions were "imported from manuscripts not used by Miss Hull or . . . Stokes [and these] sometimes increase the interest of a story amazingly."[34]

And Lady Gregory's job was difficult! The ancient Irish manuscripts of the Red Branch cycle are almost endless, and they date from the eleventh century (when the Book of the Dun Cow was recorded) and extend to the midnineteenth century. The faults of the narrative often are in the original tales themselves, not in her rendition of them; for such antics as Cuchulain's smearing his face with berries to look like a grown man with a beard are unfortunate reflections of an unsophisticated people. P. E. More correctly notes the great qualitative difference between *Cuchulain* and *Gods and Fighting Men;* he agrees with Douglas Hyde, who called the doings of the Fenians "bits of mere folklore."

It is difficult to relate Cuchulain to an historical figure or to an age or even to say with certitude whether the Red Branch Knights did indeed live before the Fianna. Although Finn and his men are even more bound up in myth than Cuchulain and his followers, it is possible to apply generally to *Cuchulain of Muirthemne* the conclusions that Lady Gregory appends to *Gods and Fighting Men.* She agrees that the bulk of Ossianic literature was in manuscripts written in Scotland from the end of the fifteenth to the middle of the seventeenth century and in Ireland from the sixteenth to the middle of the nineteenth century. But Lady Gregory is not convinced by the historical details that support the view that Finn was an actual figure living in the third century. She determined, rather, that the Finn saga was formed by an early race that occupied both Ireland and Scotland. Lady Gregory tried to build upon the foundations of the seventeenth century Annalists in order to fit the Fianna into a definite epoch; "but the whole story seemed trivial and incoherent until I began to think of them as almost contemporaneous with the Battle of Magh Tuireadh, which even the Annalists put back into mythical ages."[35] Looking beyond the anachronisms of the tales, Lady Gregory seems to have agreed with Yeats, who believed that the imaginative power of the sagas is far more important than their historicity.

Gods and Fighting Men begins suggestively with a description of the arrival of the Tuatha de Danaan, the gods of Dana, in what was later known to be Ireland. These "Men of the Dea" possessed the qualities of the Sidhe, which they became after they had gone underground. The gods of the Irish came in a mist "through the air and the high air"[36] to Ireland. Lady Gregory, who starts with these creatures, excludes other mythological settlers who preceded them.

Lady Gregory interjects some grim humor into the opening pages of *Gods and Fighting Men* as Bres of the Tuatha de Danaan meets Streng of the inimical Firbolgs (the "invaders" or "villains" of Irish myth). Each is afraid of the other's weapons; unhappily, their mutual respect and consequent negotiations could not halt war. And Bres commits the prime sin of many Irish statesmen after him; for, when he finds his tribe losing the battle, he goes to the Fomor for help and thus begins a long succession of Irish chieftains like Dervorgilla's husband who call in the outsider and eventually are forced to give part of Ireland to him.

The first third of *Gods and Fighting Men* is taken up with a rambling discussion of the deeds of several Tuatha de Danaan gods; the last two-thirds is concerned with the deeds of the Fianna, the mobile tribe of one hundred, some of whom were descended from the Tuatha de Danaan. Lady Gregory has difficulty about the contradictions within the Fenians when she blends them into her image of an idealistic Irish past group. Perhaps the Ossianic cycle became so "popular," so altered by the shifting memories of cottagers, that its original form can never be restored. Certainly, the cycle differs in intent and composition from the Ulster cycle in which Cuchulain possesses all the virtues of the Celtic warrior. Finn and his men were "extratribal" mercenaries, and Finn himself may have aided in the Irish raids on Roman Britain, despite Lady Gregory's implied denials. Throughout *Gods and Fighting Men*, Lady Gregory's efforts to glorify the Fianna succeed only in making them appear as fairy tale characters who lack stature or as untrustworthy knaves such as Finn was in his pursuit of Grania. The discrepancies may have attracted Lady Gregory to the personality of Grania, who defies the questionable Celtic "system," and to the character of Ossian, Finn's son, who returns from Tir nan Og, the land of everlasting youth, "after the Fianna" (. . . , after the Fenians have all died). Ossian is excluded from the warriors' world and is also unable to accept St. Patrick's sterile religion. The Finn saga leads to the battle with the high king of the world, which Finn wins, and, later, to Finn's defeat at the sorrowful battle of Gabhra. Lady Gregory implies that Finn's increasing tyranny made it possible for the high king finally to gain control.

The crucial segment of *Gods and Fighting Men* is the triangle of Finn, Diarmuid, and Grania. Lady Gregory, who was a champion of woman's rights in a male-dominated society, stresses that Grania's decision to marry Finn after he has tricked Diarmuid into his death is brought about by Diarmuid's lack of romantic feeling for Grania and by his preference for the companionship of the hunters to that of his wife.

Grania, daughter of the king of Ireland, is the "best in shape and size" in the world; and Finn regards her as a true prize. His courtship is unconventional by modern practice but is in keeping with the mores of his era; and, when Finn attempts to win Grania's hand by his skill with riddles, she frankly dislikes him as a prospective mate. Grania compels Diarmuid to take her away by putting bonds on him—by making him swear an oath to obey her in all things; and Lady Gregory initially suppresses Diarmuid's feelings about the affair in order to emphasize Grania's resourcefulness. All the warriors encourage Diarmuid in the "kidnapping" of Grania, although Diarmuid turns out to be somewhat wooden when he refuses their help because of his fear that Finn might harm them. Later the Fianna lose much of their stature after Finn deceives Diarmuid into fulfilling a prophecy that he will be killed by a boar and then refuses Diarmuid the water of life that could revive him.

Diarmuid's death splits loyalties in the troop, and the rest of *Gods and Fighting Men* is devoted to the fate of the individual members. But, though the Fianna is fragmented, its members are not obliterated; and the legends about them maintain that they shall return when Ireland needs them: "But some say the day will come when the Dord Fiann will be sounded three times, and that at the sound of it the Fianna will rise up as strong and as well as ever they were. And there are some say Finn, son of Cumhal, has been on the earth now and again since the old times, in the shape of one of the heroes of Ireland."[37]

The dialogue with Oisin, who has returned still young from the enchanted land, and with Saint Patrick is a fitting epilogue to the heroic tales. Patrick's attempts to convert the man who hunted with the Fianna are limpid indeed. The saint is portrayed as a sadistic as well as a doctrinaire and rigid man; he tells Oisin that Finn is in hell and that not even Oisin's dog would be able to accompany him to heaven. To his everlasting credit, Oisin prefers to take his chances with condemnation and rejects Patrick's paradise.

CHAPTER 3

Work with the Abbey Theatre

I Aims of an Irish Theatre: Preliminaries

THE Irish Literary Theatre, which grew into the Abbey Theatre, was founded on January 15, 1899, under the auspices of the National Literary Society. The role of Lady Gregory in its founding has so often been neglected that it is time to redress the balance. It is she who made Yeats's dream of an Irish theater a reality by her organizational power, by her immediate enthusiasm, and by her tact in eliciting support from all of the political and social factions of the time. She was able to "blend this oil and vinegar [Yeats and Martyn] and make them agree that the first performances of the Irish Literary Theatre . . . should consist of Edward Martyn's Ibsenitish play *The Heather Field* and Yeats's dreamily poetic play *The Countess Cathleen.*"[1] Because of the political polarizations of the era and the bitterness of personal oppositions, Lady Gregory's ability to win widespread support was "little short of marvellous."[2]

The discussions that began the Irish Literary Theatre occurred in the early months of 1897 when Yeats and Sir Alfred Lyall went to have tea at Lady Gregory's newly leased flat in Queen Anne's Mansions. After Lyall had left for an evening elsewhere, Yeats discussed his plan for building a theater somewhere in the suburbs of London to produce Romantic plays. At that time, he was assisted by Florence Farr, who shared his desire for poetic plays as opposed to paying ones. Their plans called for the production of dramas by Edward Martyn and Robert Bridges and for the solicitation of plays from Standish O'Grady and Fiona Macleod. Yeats foresaw a reaction against Realism and Ibsen; and, without fully realizing it, he was laying the foundations for the later break with Martyn and Moore and for the charge that the Abbey ignored plays dealing with the middle class.

After Lady Gregory had asked Yeats to visit Coole, he found himself in the summer of 1897 at Duras, the home located a few miles from Coole of Lady Gregory's friend and Edward Martyn's cousin, Count Florimond de Basterot. Here Lady Gregory and Yeats again spoke of the Irish Theatre project, and Yeats apparently saw an omen of success in the flock of wild ducks that always gathered to greet de Basterot's arrival from Paris to Duras. As Joseph Hone writes, "it was in the garden at Duras that the Irish National Theatre . . . was born. . . ."[3] In *The Trembling of the Veil* (1922), Yeats states that he informed Lady Gregory that lack of funds was forcing him to give up his scheme to produce plays in London. Lady Gregory had never favored his London project, and her offer to raise the money came from her desire to have a national theater in Ireland.

Earlier in the afternoon at Duras, Lady Gregory writes in *Our Irish Theatre*, "though I had never been at all interested in theatres, our talk turned on plays."[4] Martyn had written two plays which had not fared well with London producers, and he now planned to try Germany as a market, since London managers, Martyn believed, felt indifferent toward the "new drama." Lady Gregory interjected her suggestion that an Irish theater might be established to stage innovative, noncommercial plays; and, though Yeats indicated that money for such a cause might be especially hard to raise in Ireland, they "went on talking, and things seemed to grow possible as [they] talked. . . ."[5] The plan was aided by Yeats's having ready the second version of *The Countess Cathleen* and by Martyn's willingness to give up the proposed German production of *The Heather Field*. Then, too, George Moore, disenchanted by London's lack of enthusiasm for innovations in drama, grew excited about the venture; but, typically, his ardor soon decreased; in a short time, he came to believe that "to give a Literary Theatre to Dublin seemed to me like giving a mule a holiday. . . ."[6]

The plan the group formed called for the hiring of a Dublin theater and for the presentation of *The Heather Field* and *The Countess Cathleen*. Lady Gregory offered the first guarantee of twenty-five pounds, and the aims of the group were typed on the Remington typewriter that she was to use throughout her career. Lady Gregory records the purposes of the company in terms that she later found to be "a little pompous": "We propose to have performed in Dublin in the spring of every year certain Celtic and Irish plays, which whatever be their degree of excellence will be written with a high ambition, and so build up a Celtic and Irish school of dramatic literature.

We hope to find in Ireland an uncorrupted and imaginative audience trained to listen by its passion for oratory. . . . [i]n carrying out a work that is outside all the political questions that divide us."[7]

The Irish Literary Theatre asked for a guarantee fund of three hundred pounds to forward its experiment, which was to last at least three years. Some of the most charming pages in *Our Irish Theatre* describe Lady Gregory's attempts to raise the money. She turned first to the old poet, Aubrey de Vere, a "very kindly" man; and she recalls the last time she saw him at a garden party in London. What she does not allude to, of course, is the role of her social position in winning patrons from the Unionists as well as from the Nationalists; and she was able to list among her guarantors the old Fenian, John O'Leary; Dr. Mahaffy; W. E. H. Lecky; Lord Dufferin; de Vere; and many Nationalist members of Parliament.

Lady Gregory had to surmount a good deal of opposition within the Dublin artistic circles where she was assumed guilty of both patronization and political sabotage. In addition, she lost more and more of her friends among the country families when the Irish Literary Theatre and later the Abbey became embroiled in politics. From the theater's early stages, W. E. H. Lecky warned her to be wary of the revolutionary trend of the organization. Lady Gregory's feelings about her fundraising activities are summarized in her quiet statement, "I think the only actual refusals I had were from three members of the Upper House."[8]

Regrettably, all the principals who began the Irish Literary Theatre could not remain together during the great days of the Abbey to give the national theater broader scope. As a result, the Irish dramatic movement falls into two distinct parts: the dramas begun before Martyn and Moore withdrew their support; and the drama after their withdrawal which was influenced primarily by Lady Gregory and which was almost entirely concerned with folk drama. Indeed, since Lady Gregory's successful peasant plays overshadowed Yeats's poetic fantasies, she is the one who must share the credit or the blame for the direction that the dramatic movement took. In this regard, her sympathizers might maintain that what was lost in breadth was gained in depth. Although she did cost the movement the help of Moore, who had lost faith in The Independent Theatre and who was eager to support the Dublin plans, Yeats was culpable in his shortsighted desire to use materials drawn from national legends for his poetic dramas; and Martyn and Moore were

most interested in applying Ibsen to social and psychological problems. Although all four dramatists collaborated in the grotesque
production of *Diarmuid and Grania* in 1901, the last offering of the
Irish Literary Theatre, the separation of their interests was clearly
evidenced. After 1901, when Lady Gregory helped Yeats bridge the
gap between legend and folklore, the peasant play was established.
However, Yeats's ideal was not realized in the new, restrictive emphasis; and, as Boyd has stated, "Had the literary energies of the
time been concentrated, instead of scattered that Theatre would
have attracted all the talents, and doubtless folk-drama would, in
due course, have asserted its claim to existence."[9]

The Irish Literary Theatre produced the unhappy *Diarmuid and
Grania* on October 21, 1901, at the Gaiety Theatre, with F. R.
Benson's Shakespearian company; but the play is of less significance
than the curtain raiser of the evening, *Casad-an-Sugan (The Twisting of the Rope)* by Douglas Hyde, the first production on any
formal stage of a play in the Irish language. *Diarmuid and Grania* is
important only because it emphasized the necessity of having Irish
actors for the Irish Theatre movement. Although Lady Gregory
regarded her contribution to *Diarmuid and Grania* as the beginning
of her artistic contribution to the Irish Theatre—she suggested bits
of dialogue, a "sentence here and there,"[10] as Yeats dictated the plot
of the play—the spectacle of English actors garbling Hyde's Gaelic
was appalling for the members of the audience who had the misfortune to attend Hyde's *The Twisting of the Rope*.

Until the Fay brothers' departure from the Abbey in January
1908, these two remarkable actors, Frank and William Fay, filled
the theatre's need for Irish actors. The brothers had planned to go to
America to pursue an acting career, but they had been so impressed
by the possibilities of the Irish movement that they decided to join
forces with Yeats, Lady Gregory, and their colleagues. The Fays
were accustomed to putting on small farces in coffee palaces and in
burlesque houses in their spare time. The brothers were perfectly
suited to work with Yeats's early poetic plays, for they seemed to
understand almost intuitively the intonations and gestures that the
roles demanded. Then too they proved their devotion through the
mundane tasks such as building and staining the props.

Lady Gregory is often blamed for the Fays' departure and for the
Protestantism of the directors that was usually contrasted with the
Catholicism of the actors. Such a view of Lady Gregory ignores,

however, the facts of the case. Lady Gregory from the start was determined that the Abbey would be a dramatist's and not an actor's theater, and the reason for her objective was verified by the often obtuse literary appreciation of the Fays who were constantly meddling in the presentations of the dramas. Frank, for instance, believed that Synge should be "excused" his drab plays because his life had held no joy!

Joseph Holloway, in a notebook entry for October 25, 1905, described not only this aspect of Frank's actions but also how Lady Gregory demonstrated the rendering of a passage in her *The White Cockade* (which was produced December 9, 1905) to the recalcitrant actor. Lady Gregory was conducting the rehearsal of the first act and the opening scene of Act II; and Frank Fay, who was in "one of his moods . . . turned crusty and sulked."[11] He then added the supreme insult to the author, who had attempted to create Patrick Sarsfield, the noble protagonist of *The White Cockade*, in an heroic vein, when he asserted that her directions would make Sarsfield a comic figure and suggested that he would be willing to play him as such: the episode epitomizes the open hostility within the troupe. After a good deal of wrangling, Frank Fay performed the passage halfheartedly; and Holloway concludes that "Mr. Fay is like a bear with a sore head when out of temper."[12]

The Fays ended their association with the Abbey when, in a last attempt to define their roles, they insisted upon the power to create a theater that would no longer emphasize "peasant" plays. At this juncture, Lady Gregory, rightfully or wrongly, responded with an emphatic "no." And adding to the problem were the Abbey's other actors who were jealous of the Fays. The leading members believed that the brothers were monopolizing the credit due to the whole company.

Frank Fay's bitterness toward Lady Gregory never completely dissipated, and four and a half years later, in October 1912, he charged that Lady Gregory had destroyed the theatre by producing too many of her own plays; and he also implied that Lady Gregory might have had the sinister intention of sabotaging the whole project. As Fay states, " 'I . . . have counted, and will publish, the number of times the pieces of that selfish old lady have been played. I viewed her entrance into our movement with distrust from the first.' "[13]

Nevertheless, both directors and actors were working together during the first trip to London, in May 1903, that led directly to the establishment of the Abbey. The actors performed with a skill that surprised the London audiences which were packed with literary leaders who were interested in the Irish visit mainly because of Lady Gregory's social position. Outstanding critics attended performances in London of *The Hour Glass, Twenty-Five, Cathleen ni Houlihan, The Pot of Broth,* and *The Laying of the Foundations.* After the successful performances, Miss Annie Horniman, a friend of Yeats from Manchester, agreed to build a theater for the Irish players. A government patent had first to be secured; and Edward Martyn helped in the negotiations, although he was becoming more and more disenchanted with the group's stress on peasant plays. An inquiry was held on August 4, 1904; and, despite some opposition by rival theaters, who feared competition, the patent was granted to Lady Gregory (since the patentee had to be an Irish citizen). In 1905, the Irish National Theatre Society, which had been playing under Lady Gregory's patent at the Abbey Theatre, became the National Theatre Society Limited, known as "the Abbey."

The theater itself was built by combining the old Mechanics' Institute in Abbey Street with the adjacent site of the former Dublin morgue. Miss Horniman supplied an annual subsidy and gave the company the theater rent free for six years. In the patent, Lady Gregory was forbidden to permit drinking and smoking, to exhibit wild beasts, and " 'to allow women or children to be hung from the flies or fixed in positions from which they cannot release themselves.' "[14]

Lady Gregory expended her energies in diversified service to the new theater. She often elucidated the meaning of a play to a group of listeners after a performance; she helped make costumes and brought bits of wardrobe from Coole and police uniforms from the Castle, Dublin's Police Headquarters; she fed the company during lean days by lugging her famous barmbracks (large plum cakes) from Gort. She often tried to encourage the audience by going out the stage door after the curtain was up and returning to the auditorium by the front hall, "hoping that in the dimness I might pass for a new arrival and so encourage the few scattered people in the stalls."[15] One of Lady Gregory's hardest tasks was reading the submitted manuscripts of plays; and, if she had not so assiduously done her work, O'Casey's plays might never have appeared.

In 1909, Lady Gregory was worn out, Yeats reported, with her creative work and translations and with her struggle in 1909 to keep Shaw's *Blanco Posnet* from being suppressed. In one of Yeats's most appreciative judgments of Lady Gregory, he writes, "Lady Gregory had brought herself to death's door with overwork, to give us, while neglecting no other duty, enough plays, translated or original, to keep the Theatre alive. . . ."[16] Yeats was indignant at the ubiquitous whispering that claimed that Lady Gregory took advantage of her position as Abbey director.

II *Defense of Synge: in Dublin and in America*

By far the greatest problem that faced the Abbey was the controversy over John Millington Synge's *The Playboy of the Western World*. The first night of the play was January 26, 1907; and the audience, at the use of the word "shift" by Christy Mahon, the play's protagonist, broke into disorder at this reference to a woman's undergarment and began the confrontation between the Abbey Theatre and the religious and political leaders of Dublin. Although the reaction to the conflict was that in Ireland "traditional symbols" are "not symbols but realities,"[17] the battle over *The Playboy* had been foreshadowed in the attack upon Synge's *In the Shadow of the Glen* when it had been presented at the Royalty Theatre on March 26, 1903. At that time, the attack had been confined to newspapers, led by the *Independent*, which charged that the author had maligned Ireland's womanhood. From 1903 on, the organ of Sinn Fein, *The United Irishman*, criticized almost every play presented by the national theater; and it added the accusation of immorality to the merely political innuendoes that had been directed at the Irish Literary Theatre since its inception. The paper was especially hostile toward Synge, whom it considered to be a French-influenced decadent; and these charges had been so significant that "immorality" had been one of the objections brought against the Abbey's application for its patent.

In fairness to jingoists of 1907, however, it must be admitted that Synge's *Playboy* could have been construed as an effective argument against Home Rule for the Irish during a period in which anything detrimental to Ireland was parsimoniously garnered by her enemies. Also, *The Playboy* seemed to revive the stage Irishman to those who could not recognize Synge's beautiful, grim humor or who could not tolerate the strong draught of unrelenting honesty in the play. At the start, for example, Christy Mahon, the diminutive hero, wanders into a village pub near Mayo and tells an admiring group that he has killed his father. Synge introduces an undercurrent of horror into his work as Pegeen Mike, the innkeeper's daughter, who later falls in love with Christy, is fascinated by the crime and tempts Christy to reveal all its macabre details: "You never hanged him [Christy's father], the way Jimmy Farrell hanged his dog from the license, and had it screeching and wiggling three hours at the butt of a string, and himself swearing it was a dead dog, and the peelers swearing it had life?"[18] Pegeen's remark about the police is matched later by the outspoken comment that caused trouble in Establishment circles: "if I'd that lad [Christy] in the house, I wouldn't be fearing the looséd kharki cut-throats [British soldiers], or the walking dead."[19]

Blended with the "abuse" to Ireland's image of the pure lass is Synge's ridicule of the false idealism behind much of the folklore movement. His picture of Widow Quin contrasts sharply with Lady Gregory's gentle prodding of the peasants' gullibility in her Irish myths. Pegeen at one point tells Christy of Widow Quin's leaking thatch that grows more pasture for her buck goat than does her square of fields. In addition, the widow, Pegeen reveals, once nursed a lamb at her breast; and Pegeen questions whether the "Lord Bishop of Connaught felt the elements of a Christian, and he eating it after in a kidney stew?"[20] This kind of humor shocked Catholic audiences in Dublin, but Synge remained indifferent to the commotion. He pursued an artistic course based upon a sincere interpretation of his findings in Western Ireland and in the Aran Islands, and he let others work out the social implications of his plays.

Lady Gregory perceived the great literary worth of Synge's *Playboy* and viewed its presentation in Dublin and in America as a victory over mob violence. After the curtain had come down during one disturbance, she insisted that the actors play until the end even though not a word was audible. She was determined to stage the play during the announced week even as she was later, in 1909, to wage war against Castle censorship and possible loss of the Abbey's patent to stage Shaw's *Blanco Posnet*. (In 1909, her defense won the lifelong friendship of Shaw; and, because of her opposition to the

English censor, she regained some of the Nationalist support lost during the *Playboy* riots.) The kind of intellectual censorship that Lady Gregory hated is seen in her anecdote about the widow of a writer of Irish plays who was permitted to produce a play only after it had been "cut and rearranged by a local committee, made up of the shopkeepers of the town."[21]

An interesting conclusion to the whole affair of *The Playboy* is found in Miss Ellis-Fermor's allusion to *The Sunday Independent*'s praise of the fact that, after the last performance of the play in Dublin, the curtain fell to " 'thunders of applause.' "[22] Andrew Malone adds, however, that the play had never been heard! Indeed, to get a hearing for Synge's play was one of the reasons behind Lady Gregory's persistent defense of *The Playboy* in America.

In July 1911, after a highly popular stay of *The Playboy* at the Court Theatre, the Abbey received an offer of an American tour from Liebler and Company, theatrical agents. The terms were excellent and included a guarantee of all expenses and thirty-five percent of the profits. One stipulation, however, was that *The Playboy* be one of the offerings. The agents were governed not by the play's artistry but by the notoriety to which it had given birth four years previously in Dublin. Since Yeats refused to spend the four months required to take the group through the United States, he, before setting out with Lennox Robinson and the company, secured Lady Gregory's word that she would follow him a week later, on the next boat, and assume management of the group.

Yeats's task in America was easy. For the first two weeks after the tour opened in the Plymouth Theatre in Boston, only a few people came to the performances. Within a week after Lady Gregory's arrival, however, the Gaelic societies marshalled their forces to castigate Lady Gregory and Lennox Robinson as anti-Christian authors and as co-conspirators against Home Rule. These denunciations were the first in a long series of attacks that greeted *The Playboy*, with diminishing force, during each of the American tours. The fight for *The Playboy* cost Lady Gregory and Yeats the slender reputation they had among Irish-Americans and drove them more and more to the moneyed and "educated" circles in the United States. Harvard University, inspired by Professor Baker's drama classes, was already familiar with Lady Gregory's plays; and the Harvard boys did their share to stamp out opposition to the play as they reenacted a scene (with the cruder parts expunged) that the students from Trinity College had put on in Dublin in 1907. As Lady Gregory writes, "There was a little booing and hissing, but there were a great many Harvard boys among the audience and whenever there was a sign of coming disapproval they cheered enough to drown it."[23]

Lady Gregory's determination to complete the tour was another victory in her battle against censorship. Although she decided early in the trip that *The Playboy* would have a hearing despite the yawp of the mob, she was almost entirely without support. Yeats was little help as he stayed at home brooding guiltily over the accounts of the tour from the newspapers and from Lady Gregory's letters. And the Dublin populace teamed up with their American friends to exaggerate the disturbances and to dredge up the old charges about the Abbey's immorality.

The ungracious conduct of Dublin occasioned Lady Gregory's writing *Our Irish Theatre* (1913), which she began as soon as she returned home in 1912 in order to correct the misinformation disseminated by rumor and the press. Given the dire circumstances behind the book's composition, little wonder that *Our Irish Theatre* emphasizes the disorder of the trip. One is surprised that Lady Gregory recorded in it any joy in the midst of disappointment. The book, dedicated to her grandson, Richard, and dated July 24, 1913, ends, however, on a happy note: "I had but just written these last pages and put together these letters when in last Christmas week we set out again for America. We spent there the first four months of this year, but this time there were no riots. . . ."[24]

Two of the most interesting episodes occurred in Chicago and in Philadelphia, where the players were arrested on charges of immorality concerning *The Playboy*. They were bailed out with five thousand dollars and had to appear before a magistrate to answer the accusations. In Philadelphia, a complaint to the authorities by any citizen could stop a play's performance, and in this instance the complaint came from a liquor salesman who, under cross-examination, revealed that he had not read a line of the work. Perhaps he was as astute as the woman who quizzed Lady Gregory about the notoriety of *The "Cowboy" of the Western World*.

In keeping with Lady Gregory's ability to find the absurd in human pretentiousness, she emphasized the foolishness of the whole Philadelphia episode; and she preferred to spend her time relating the charming experience of her lecture on playwriting that was given in that city. She was told just before beginning her talk that several dramatists were in the room. She overcame the nervousness which she usually felt before a speech by apologizing on the ground of "an inferior cook being flattered at being asked to give recipes, whereas a real *chef* keeps the secrets to himself."[25]

Her experience in Chicago, by contrast, was more dangerous. Once, when getting back to her hotel, she found a death threat written in vile language; and it was accompanied by a picture of a coffin and a pistol that were to warn her that she would not live to see Connemara again. (In *Our Irish Theatre*, Lady Gregory reproduces the letter, with all its misspellings and its crude drawing.) In Chicago, she insisted upon walking to the theater each night without police protection . . . usually alone. This act of bravery was in one sense the highlight of Lady Gregory's career as an organizer. After the return to Dublin, the Abbey Theatre became more and more a people's theater as Realism took the place of legendary materials. Subsequent trips to America never really paid the expenses. Lady Gregory fought a successful battle in America; but, in winning, she ended a glorious war, for *The Playboy* was no longer a topic of bitter controversy.

Lady Gregory's direct influence upon Synge's writings was minimal, and his generous acknowledgment of her importance exaggerates his need for her assistance. Synge, a solitary and a scholar, had mastered a brand of Gaelic-English before Lady Gregory had devised her Kiltartan, just as Hyde had done before 1893. Synge appreciated her popularization of the idiom and her wide demonstration that the dialect was flexible enough to appeal to a vast and discriminating audience. His generosity stemmed also from the deep sympathy Lady Gregory had toward the eccentricities of his genius, even though she was suspicious of its effects in the plays, which seemed not immediately to add dignity to her country—the avowed purpose of the Irish Theatre movement. Lady Gregory perceptively distinguished between Synge's artistic talents and his direct social relevance—or lack of it—and she felt at times an almost immaterial bond of affection with him. Yeats records that she quaked with depression on the morning of the day on which Synge died, for she had guessed that some terrible event was about to happen. But Synge is important in a chronicle of Lady Gregory's contributions primarily because, in defending his masterpiece in America, she appeared as the central organizational power of the Abbey.

III Influence upon Yeats

The myth perpetrated by Oliver Gogarty, who alleged that Yeats had written the best of Lady Gregory's works, has been shown to be the opposite of the truth. Actually, Lady Gregory helped Yeats to write all of his plays before he started the Noh Theatre under Ezra Pound's influence in 1917 with At the Hawk's Well, and she played a great part in providing Realistic dialogue for his Stories of Red Hanrahan (1904). As Ann Saddlemyer states, "if we take Yeats's word alone it is clear that very few of his plays were written without her advice and actual contribution, beginning with Cathleen ni Houlihan. . . . and ending in 1928 with his translation of King Oedipus. . . ."[26] Yeats, a poet, sought the assistance of his patroness, who helped him climb down from his window of high idealism and who assisted him in putting his dramatic fables into common speech: "he wanted to come closer to the folk, and so projected that version in peasant idiom of the Red Hanrahan stories, which he was to make . . . in partnership with Lady Gregory."[27] Lady Gregory refused to accept credit for the playwriting with Yeats because her intent from the beginning was to build the Irish theater around Yeats. In addition, simply too many plays in the early years were written by Lady Gregory "without unnecessarily appending her name to a whole block of others."[28] Moreover, Lady Gregory always jealously guarded Yeats's reputation; and she could never tolerate his sharing fame, even with the acting crew that helped the Abbey begin its career. In short, Lady Gregory helped to define Yeats's style, dramatic construction, and techniques of characterization.

Certain Kiltartan mannerisms in plays ascribed to Yeats show the dominance of Lady Gregory's language in the speech of the characters. These include the employment of the present progressive in phrases and clauses where it would not ordinarily occur; the omnipresence of the neuter pronoun "it" with the linking verb, "to be," "in idiomatic structures preceding what would normally be the main verb . . .";[29] the use of modifying clauses in place of phrases; and the employment of the passive progressive and the passive infinitive. Added to the list must be the ever-recurrent reflexive pronoun and such peculiarities of speech as the phrase "in it."

Lady Gregory's influence is especially evident in *The Unicorn from the Stars* (1908), which Yeats claims should have been signed by Lady Gregory, so great was her part in the work; in *Cathleen ni Houlihan* (1902), in which all except the heroine's speeches are probably Lady Gregory's work; and in *The Pot of Broth* (1904), which Yeats supplied as a farce for the Fays. Traces of Lady Gregory's Kiltartan can be found, in addition, in *The King's Threshold* (1904); in the dialect spoken by the sailors in *The Shadowy Waters* (1900); and in countless passages of *The Hour-Glass* (1903) and of *Deirdre* (1907). In *The King's Threshold*, Lady Gregory is responsible for much of the dialogue of the Mayor, the cripples, and the Chorus. Lady Gregory helped Yeats to write *On Baile's Strand* (1903), moreover, and to rewrite one of his Oedipus plays. She supplied, finally, the mythological basis for at least three of Yeats's plays: *On Baile's Strand* is taken from "The Only Son of Aoife" in *Cuchulain of Muirthemne*; Yeats's *Deirdre* is based upon Lady Gregory's version of that legend; and *The Golden Helmet* (1908) came from Lady Gregory's rendering of "The Feast of Bricriu." Lady Gregory's research in folklore unearthed so much prime material that it is no wonder that Edward Martyn as well as Yeats and Synge used some of it. Martyn formed his Peg Inerny, a central character in *Maeve* (1899), upon Lady Gregory's findings.

In *Cathleen ni Houlihan*, the human base for the heroine's high idealism is seen in her assertion that any young man must be willing to die for her; and this view is provided by Lady Gregory in the chatter of Peter, the father of the bridegroom Michael, and Peter's wife Bridget. In the best "workhouse ward" style, Bridget says, after being chided by her husband, "What had you the day I married you but a flock of hens and you feeding them, and a few lambs and you driving them to the market at Ballina?"[30]

Lady Gregory's enthusiasm for helping Yeats with *The Pot of Broth* came from her interest in the Irish Theatre movement and not from any confidence in the inconsequential curtain raiser. She expended a great deal of attention on the slight piece because it was needed by the Fays' acting troupe—although Yeats seems to have taken the play more seriously: "I gave Fay a little farce, *The Pot of Broth*, written with Lady Gregory's help but showing that neither Lady Gregory nor I could yet distinguish between the swift-moving dialect—the dialect of the Irish novelists no matter what part of Ireland they wrote of—and the slow-moving country dialect."[31] At its worst, *The Pot of Broth* reveals the unhappy combination of what Yeats considered peasant speech with the language that Lady Gregory had mastered in her Kiltartan. Of such is the lame dialogue of Sibby when she asks, "Why couldn't the Kernans have given the priest his dinner the way they always do? What did it matter their mother's brother to have died?"[32] Nevertheless, in his notes to *The Pot of Broth,* Yeats does formulate a valid appraisal of Lady Gregory's assistance to him in all of his playwriting: " 'I hardly know how much of the play is my work, for Lady Gregory helped me as she has helped in every play of mine where there is dialect, and sometimes where there is not. In those first years of the theatre we all helped one another . . . but certainly I was the most indebted as I had no mastery of speech that purported to be of real life. This play may be more Lady Gregory's than mine, for I remember once urging her to include it in her own work, and her refusing to do so.' "[33]

In *On Baile's Strand,* Lady Gregory helped in the creation of the malevolent Fool and the evil Blind Man; but they also reflect Yeats's scorn of the underling who pursues his own greedy ambitions while remaining indifferent to the fate of the Leader. In the play, Yeats adds two elements to his source, Lady Gregory's *Cuchulain of Muirthemne.* First, he makes Cuchulain resemble the pietistic Brian Boru seen in *Kincora* (1905) in his desire for peace and in his willingness to accept Conchubar as king out of social pressures. Second, he explains Cuchulain's killing of his son by letting it be known that the youth has challenged the entire court and that, consequently, Cuchulain must uphold its honor. Conversely, a most unfortunate blending of the divergent literary techniques of Yeats and Lady Gregory is found in *The Unicorn from the Stars*; and one is forced to agree that the play is "the kind of thing where . . . it is impossible to get good results out of collaboration. Lady Gregory's peasant characters were not good exponents of Mr. Yeats's mysticism, which on this occasion was more than usually tenebrous."[34]

It must be admitted, therefore, that Lady Gregory did little to make Yeats's plays theatrical successes. Fortunately, she saw that her purposes and talents were different from Yeats's; and she was able to go her own artistic way, relying upon Yeats for advice, but not depending upon his collaboration. Yeats's greatest use of Kiltartanlike speech, ironically, is found in the homey, integrated poetry of his later years when he blended many influences, including Lady

Gregory's, to voice in language common to men his own bruised idealism.

Lady Gregory's greater service to Yeats came in her patronage, in her unending devotion to her vision of Yeats's genius. By supplying him with the use of Coole, Lady Gregory enabled Yeats's poetic techniques to develop; and, by adding her moderating personality to his, she allowed him to steer a steady course through crisis after crisis. The relationship hurt Lady Gregory artistically by stunting her desire for freer expression and experimentation; but it did give her her raison d'être: Yeats was Lady Gregory's "cause" before the death of her nephew, Hugh Lane, and the controversy over his will; and, by 1916, Yeats and the Abbey had been "launched."

Lady Gregory's first task in providing a base of Realism for Yeats's abstractions was to wean him away from magic. As Katherine Tynan states, "he veered steadily towards magic, from which, however, he has long since got away since Lady Gregory's friendship began to throw its protecting influence over him."[35] Lady Gregory's task was difficult: before coming to Coole, Yeats pondered the possible validity of folk tales, since, he felt, they were supported by a great amount of testimony. One night he awoke in a state of paralysis to hear an incantation being delivered through his lips; the experience helped Yeats formulate his theory of the mask. Lady Gregory gave a sympathetic ear to Yeats's visions, even though she found little meaning in the mysticism surrounding the Celtic twilight. From the start, her objectivity corrected Yeats's practice of using the Celtic notion to deposit all "the necromantic ideas with which he had saturated himself . . ."[36] by blending them with the superstitious practices of the cottagers. In Lady Gregory's hands, Rosa Alchemica became a homely herb and the uninhibited "Red O'Hanrahan" turned into the "serious steady dancing of a hornpipe on the Abbey stage."[37]

Not only in his autobiographical *Dramatis Personae* (1936) does Yeats damn Lady Gregory with faint praise; his neglect is seen in his editing of the *Oxford Book of Modern Verse (1892–1935)*, in which he includes only some translations by her from Hyde's Irish. When Lady Gregory did receive Yeats's public praise, moreover, it was usually based upon extraneous qualities often chosen to support one of Yeats's own theses. Yeats found greatness in Lady Gregory's translations of Molière (another of her minor achievements), but he demonstrated that Molière was readily adaptable to Catholic countries, which love fun for its own sake and which do not demand a moral sting in a literary work.

Yeats partially redeemed himself during Lady Gregory's last sickness in the winter of 1930–1931. Lady Gregory was now almost eighty and apparently dying; Yeats stayed in Ireland to see her through her worst moments. But even here the debt was not fully paid: Yeats at the time needed the rest almost as much as Lady Gregory. After her death, Yeats seems to have placed as much stress upon the loss of Coole as upon the passing of his benefactress. His failure to write any new verse stemmed then from his fear that his imaginative faculties may have been arrested by the deterioration of the Coole estate and by emotions numbed by the loss of its traditions. His comment to Mrs. Shakespear concerning Lady Gregory's death epitomizes the distance that he had managed in a short time to place between himself and her memory. Lapsing into his old tendency to value human beings for their tenacity and firmness of purpose, he states, " 'She was her indomitable self to the last. . . .' "[38]

IV *Two More Defenses of Freedom*

Lady Gregory's battle for Shaw's *Blanco Posnet* shows the way in which she was taking more and more the lead in the defense of the Abbey. The theater's production of Shaw's play grew out of a visit of Lady Gregory in the summer of 1909 to Ayot St. Lawrence. Shaw gave her *The Shewing-up of Blanco Posnet* to read, and Lady Gregory was so impressed by the work that she decided to stage it. Her reaction to the play was put into one word: " 'Hypocrites.' "[39] Lady Gregory was not at all disturbed by the supposed blasphemy of Blanco's sermon, "his challenge to the divinity." She writes, "I saw that Blanco's sermon, coming as it did after bustling action, was in danger of seeming monotonous."[40] She made the lead actor deliver the first section standing atop a bench, then brought him down to present some of the speech sitting on a table, and after that directed him to speak some of the words directly to Elder Posnet: "After that I sent him with a leap on to the table for the last phrases."[41]

The tangle about the play occurred because the English censor's writ, which had banned *Blanco Posnet* in England, did not apply in Ireland; for theatrical laws for Ireland were legislated in the old Irish Parliament. Because of a flaw in the Abbey's patent, however, Lord

Lieutenant Aberdeen was empowered to forbid the performance in Dublin; and he tried to persuade Lady Gregory to cancel the play whose performance date by that time had been announced. Lady Gregory never disclosed the substance of her interview with Lord Aberdeen; and, although Yeats and Lady Gregory fully believed that the Abbey's patent would be taken away—they were threatened by a telegram from Dublin Castle—they presented the play to a crowded house on August 26, 1909. The audience, including a large contingent from the Castle, sat quietly through the play and waited for the nonexistent heretical parts to be spoken. When it was finished, they broke into applause; for the Dubliners saluted more the political than the artistic event of *Blanco Posnet.*

Lady Gregory gives an intriguing account of her conference with the lord lieutenant, who tried to avoid the confrontation by initially shifting her to a minion. To this representative, she explained the impossibility of cancelling the announced play: the troupe would be suspected of " 'having tried to produce something bad and injurious. . . .' "[42] Lady Gregory decided to go on with the play and "die gloriously" if die she must. The only part of the conversation with the lord lieutenant that she reveals is his offer of a cup of tea which, despite her thirst following a dusty railway journey, she refused lest she compromise her principles by accepting a bribe. When *Blanco Posnet* was staged as the special attraction of the Abbey during Horse Show Week, it won back many of the theater's active sympathizers.

One of the most perplexing events in the Abbey's chronicle is the series of machinations which led to Miss Annie Horniman's decision to withdraw her subsidy from the theater in November 1910. Since Lady Gregory is often blamed for driving away the delicate and supposedly innocuous Miss Horniman, it might be well to examine the tangle of relationships whose climax occurred early in May 1910, when the inexperienced manager, Lennox Robinson, kept the Abbey open on the occasion of Edward VII's sudden death. Because Robinson did not understand the interplay of politics and art, he saw nothing wrong with allowing the Abbey to operate. He grew apprehensive, however, when he learned that all other theaters had closed. At this juncture, Robinson sent a telegram to Lady Gregory at Coole asking her advice; but the messenger boy was a Nationalist who was later honored for his patriotic gesture of delaying the telegram, even though he lost his job. The lad took three hours to cover the three miles from Gort to Coole and to return to the post office. As a result of his delay in delivering the telegram, Lady Gregory's reply suggesting that the Abbey close through courtesy was not received until the matinee was in progress. Robinson admits that he too was responsible for producing Padraic Colum's Realistic workhouse play, *Thomas Muskerry*, and that his interest in the work caused him to ignore the death of Edward VII.

Miss Horniman's action was immediate and decisive. On May 10, 1910, she telegraphed Lady Gregory to tell her that she had found the opening of the theater on the previous Saturday to be disgraceful and to warn her that a performance on the day of the funeral would automatically stop her subsidy. She demanded Robinson's dismissal and an apology in the Dublin press. Lady Gregory not only refused to comply with the request for the firing of Robinson but also issued a deliberately ambiguous "apology" to the newspapers: " 'regret that owing to accident the theatre remained open.' "[43] Lady Gregory's motives were twofold: she was unwilling to sacrifice the inexperienced but talented Robinson, although she did not grant him a directorship until 1923; and she deeply resented the commotion Miss Horniman was making over a trivial incident, a stir that cost Lady Gregory a new endowment that she was seeking from the Unionist camp. But to Miss Horniman, Robinson's act was one more attempt to wave the green flag over the Abbey.

When Miss Horniman withdrew her subsidy from the Irish National Theatre, she turned over all her rights in the Abbey for the minor sum of one thousand pounds, and a private Limited Liability Company was formed to deal with the finances. Synge died in 1909, and the company carried on with only two directors until the selection of Robinson. Having learned their lesson, Yeats and Lady Gregory refused to finance the Abbey by soliciting shareholders; instead, they asked that an endowment fund of five thousand pounds be created with voluntary gifts.

CHAPTER 4

Comedies

I Seven Short Plays (1909)

THE career of Lady Gregory, playwright, began, therefore, with Yeats as far back as 1901 when she contributed ruggedly humorous parts for *Where There Is Nothing* (later to be entitled *The Unicorn from the Stars*), *Cathleen ni Houlihan*, and *The Pot of Broth*. Her attitude toward her contributions was invariably humble, although she did reveal her assistance to Yeats in *Our Irish Theatre* and in her notes to a few of her plays. Her statement, "because you have taught me my trade,"[1] must be taken in the generous sense in which it was intended. By 1909, Lady Gregory, in the midst of her great creative decade, could afford to patronize a man whose plays were proving much less popular than hers and whose organizational functions were being relinquished more and more to her. The statement to Yeats was made in the same self-denigrating vein as Lady Gregory's given reason for beginning her career—her desire to provide comic relief from the somber Yeatsean dramas, which, at any rate, did not fill an evening.

From this stated intention came Lady Gregory's sentimental *Twenty-Five*, which was at first rejected by the Fays in September 1902 because of its weak structure—it centers in a card game difficult to stage—and because an emigrant character returns to Ireland with one hundred pounds and thus, according to the Fays, encouraged emigration. The play was produced over the brothers' veto, at Molesworth Hall, on March 14, 1903, during the fourth series of the Irish National Theatre Society's performances. Even so, Lady Gregory did not include the work in her first collection of short plays and said only that one of the seven pieces, *The Jackdaw* (1907), was written to obliterate the mistakes of *Twenty-Five* by making "humour lay the ghost of sentiment."[2] Another short play that preceded *Twenty-Five* is the pietistic *My First Play*, written early in 1902, about the legend of Colman and Guaire; it was never performed and not published until 1930.

Lady Gregory's plays, whether folk histories or comedies, have never been thoroughly evaluated. However, Miss Elizabeth Coxhead, approaching the plays from a novelist's point of view, and Ann Saddlemyer and Hazard Adams, analyzing them in perceptive but brief essays, have partially dispelled the shadow that Yeats casts over Lady Gregory. This chapter assesses the contributions that Lady Gregory's comedies have made to English and Irish literature, indicates her suggestive speech patterns, and discusses her use of symbols. The intent is not to "defend" Lady Gregory's works, the mistake usually made in approaching her plays, but to define their worth.

The imagined need to defend Lady Gregory stems in part from her method of combining theory with dramatic practice. She had little abstract basis behind her work; and, when she did theorize, as about the distinction between comedy and tragedy, her views seem shallow. Because Lady Gregory did not philosophize about the essence and purpose of playwriting, the grace and the ease of her lines were often regarded as simplistic. Miss Ellis-Fermor perpetuates this view of Lady Gregory's plays without meaning to do so: "[S]he never has a theory about how a thing is to be done until she comes to do it. Then, a few notes, a diagram or two in different coloured pencils, the sudden synthesis of one or two reminiscences or dreams, and the play shapes, as often as not into a comedy when she meant a tragedy, or with the main figure a character she had not intended to appear."[3] Miss Ellis-Fermor generalizes about the spontaneity of Lady Gregory's dramatic purposes from only one significant source, Lady Gregory's notes to her first hit, *Spreading the News* (1904), which began in a somber vein and developed humorously. Miss Ellis-Fermor was influenced by Lady Gregory's admission that her characters "put out feet" and take their own way once they find paper. In *Spreading the News*, however, the main character, Bartley Fallon, shows a skillful blend of comic and tragic elements and becomes a carefully etched picaro.

An examination of the form of Lady Gregory's plays, moreover, demonstrates that only infrequently did she lose control of her material. Though the characters are sometimes garrulous, there is no need either to emphasize this one fact or to excuse it on the grounds that Lady Gregory's assistance to Yeats lessened the tautness of her plays. One can agree that Lady Gregory's plays often resemble comic fantasies built like houses of cards, but one does not need to concur with the stress that Miss Ellis-Fermor places upon the effect of Lady Gregory's wordiness: "Sometimes the action seems to drag a little as in parts of *Hyacinth Halvey, The Jackdaw,* or *The Image.* . . ."[4] The three plays are quite different in the type of creation each was intended to be.

Spreading the News (1904) is the first work to appear in *Seven Short Plays* (1909) since it is the first play in the collection to have been produced by the Abbey Theatre Company; the others in the volume are *Hyacinth Halvey* (1906), *The Rising of the Moon* and *The Jackdaw* (1907), *The Workhouse Ward* (1908), *The Travelling Man* (1910), and *The Gaol Gate* (1906). Played at the opening of the Abbey on December 27, 1904, *Spreading the News* followed Yeats's *On Baile's Strand.* Lady Gregory heard her otherwise successful play attacked on the basis that the Irish are not such gossips as she presents; but she was able to assert some time later that the Abbey audiences had been educated to realize that "[a] play is a selection not a photograph."[5]

Spreading the News traces the misadventures that befall the protagonist, Bartley Fallon, at an Irish fair; and his problems are caused by the eagerness of the villagers to spread gossip. Bartley follows his acquaintance, Jack Smith, to return Jack's hayfork, which Smith has inadvertently left behind at the apple stall of the half deaf Mrs. Tarpey whose misinterpretations are the chief source of the rumors that form the basis of the play. Just before Bartley leaves, he trips and spills a basket of apples; and his bungling objectively correlates with the series of complications about to begin. Shortly after, Mrs. Fallon says that her husband has gone after Jack Smith with a hayfork, when he has actually gone to return the implement. Mrs. Tarpey next is told that Mrs. Smith is laying out a sheet on a hedge, and she thinks she hears: "Laying out a sheet for the dead!"[6]

The villagers then assume that Bartley has been having an affair with Mrs. Smith and wanted Jack out of the way. Their concern as the rumor spreads is with the ability of Bartley to support Mrs. Smith. Bartley is arrested and charged with murder; he is handcuffed, beleaguered by his wife, and incurs the wrath of Smith, who believes the stories about the cheating. As the buffoonlike policemen go to look for the "real" Jack Smith, Bartley muses about his possible fate. He feels that, if he and Smith are put in the cell for the night, the cuffs will be taken off the "aggrieved" husband and that murder will surely be committed.

The "point" of *Spreading the News* depends upon verbal tricks, but it is realized also through a complex of closely articulated events. The plot is deftly structured, with the overturned basket of apples and the presence of police at the fairgrounds lending credence to the web of imagined events, as does the song, "The Red-haired Man's Wife." Bartley is accused of killing the red-haired Smith and of having an affair with Smith's wife; and, at the end of the play, even after the plot has been partially untangled, Bartley has still to look forward to a dreadful night in jail with the "resurrected" Smith, who naively believes the rumors about his wife's infidelity. Also, mistakes made in the opening dialogue of the police officials lead easily into the series of blunders that Mrs. Tarpey is about to perpetrate. The magistrate's misinterpretation of his subordinate's words allows him to believe that murder is common at the fair and foreshadows Bartley Fallon's fear at the end of the play that Smith might really murder him.

Spreading the News is sprinkled with allegory. Ireland is Eden, in which apples are spilled and in which gossip poisons the Garden of the Fair Green. The magistrate, who learned his trade in the Andaman Islands, is a satiric picture of a colonizer, perhaps one resembling an underling of Sir William Gregory when he was the governor of Ceylon. And the confusion over religion in the play is Lady Gregory's comment about Irish theological stratification. The magistrate's openings words score England's deprecating attitude toward the Irish: "So that is the Fair Green. Cattle and sheep and mud. No system. What a repulsive sight!" (15). And later, when a character appears smoking a pipe, Lady Gregory once again calls attention to the Establishment's ignorance of the Irish and their national color: "The smoke from that man's pipe had a greenish look; he may be growing unlicensed tobacco at home" (16).

Lady Gregory's initial purpose in writing the play is quite different from its embodiment. The idea first came to her "as a tragedy." She visualized people sitting about and watching as a sprightly lass went to market. In the evening, she saw the same girl returning sadly and others turning from her; a word had been dropped that had destroyed her "name." Lady Gregory explains, however, that the Abbey needed comedy and not tragedy to augment and counter the "high poetic" works of Yeats.

Lady Gregory's comments about her artistic dilemma over Bartley Fallon demonstrate her pride in her work and her ability to structure a characterization. In the beginning, she could imagine Bartley only as dull-witted and as not fit for the punishment of handcuffs. Then one day at Duras she met a melancholy man who told her his troubles, "'But I'm thinking if I went to America, its [sic] long ago to-day I'd be dead. And it's a great expense for a poor man to be buried in America.' "[7] The observation, tragicomic in essence, led to Lady Gregory's characterization of Bartley, whom she tried to provide with one glorious day of misfortune. (Bartley's words about the expensiveness of living in America show, too, that Lady Gregory has learned her lesson since *Twenty-Five:* his attitude would hardly lead to emigration.) And Fallon is not merely pitiable. His "dead-pan" attitudes anticipate later "method" acting techniques and some recent underplayed comedy routines: "Handcuffs now! Glory be! I always said, if there was ever any misfortune coming to this place it was on myself it would fall."[8] So popular did the play prove that companies other than the Abbey often used it; and, as Lady Gregory says, "Boers have done me the honour of translating and pirating it."[9]

In *Hyacinth Halvey,* presented at the Abbey on January 19, 1906, Lady Gregory once more experiments with technique: she tries to put artistic distance between herself and her source for Halvey, a well-groomed youth who was pointed out to Lady Gregory in the Abbey's stalls. Because of some gossip about the young man, Lady Gregory wondered if a respectable bearing and good name might not often be a burden. He became Hyacinth when Lady Gregory decided that one "must set one's original a little way off to get a translation rather than a tracing. . . ."[10]

Hyacinth Halvey concerns a young man who arrives in Cloon with such glowing recommendations that he is asked to perform several obnoxious duties, ones suitable to a youth of high moral standards. The townspeople insist that he lecture on the spiritual regeneration of the farmers, wear a teetotaler's button, and live in a room where he can be constantly watched by the parish priest. He is to be denied all privacy; for, it is inferred, Hyacinth has such an irreproachable character that he never lowered the shades in his room. The second movement of the play deals with Hyacinth's failing attempts to extricate himself from the situation occasioned by the letters attesting to his character. The play could have ended with his unsuccessful effort to incriminate himself by stealing a sheep; for the last segment of the work, which concerns the attempts of Hyacinth and a messenger boy to rob a church, seems tacked on. When the lad is accused, Hyacinth takes the blame, is described as a greater saint than ever before, and is thoroughly trapped in the town.

The play opens at Cloon's Post Office with the omnipresent Mrs. Delane telling Quirke, the butcher, that the new sub-sanitary inspector, Hyacinth Halvey, is due to arrive that day. He carries, she swears, three pounds of "testimonials." In the meantime, the department of agriculture is sending a lecturer to the town "in furtherance of the moral development of the rural classes";[11] and, when the lecturer is unable to come, the sergeant suggests that Hyacinth, because of his fine credentials, might take his place. In an effort to destroy his own good name, Hyacinth enlists the aid of the half-witted messenger boy; but the lad is an incompetent: he lacks the philosophical basis of Bartley Fallon's characterization. He becomes an inexpert foil in the attempt to help Hyacinth ruin his reputation. And Halvey's machinations are no more effective; for, when he steals Quirke's sheep, he really saves the butcher whose meat is about to be confiscated: there having been too many complaints from the Shannon Fort Barracks.

Some of Lady Gregory's wittiest dialogue is found in *Hyacinth Halvey*. She explains the lecturer's absenteeism: he was detained holding an inquest over a drake. And she allows Quirke to describe vividly the sheep that was almost seized: "Gone all to nothing. . . . It did not weigh as much as a lamb of two months . . . . The ribs of it streaky with the dint of patent medicines . . ." (45). There is a good deal of humor, as well, in the trapping of the hero whose letters are all forgeries; and, in subsequent allusions to police and military, Lady Gregory becomes the social critic who attacks English interests as well as stringent Roman Catholicism:

MISS JOYCE: You will be near to the Sergeant in the lodging I speak of. The house is convenient to the barracks.
HYACINTH: *(doubtfully.)* To the barracks?
MISS JOYCE: Alongside of it and the barrack yard behind. And that's not all. It is opposite to the priest's house. (38)

In addition, Lady Gregory adds a bit of salt to her description of Cloon's villagers by comments such as Mrs. Delane's about the

moral development of a girl she once knew who had lost her character: "she washed her feet in a blessed well after, and it [the well]
dried up on the minute" (35). And the dead sheep at the side of
Quirke's door becomes symbolic of Halvey, who is "executed" by the
opaque community.

Lady Gregory places Hyacinth in Cloon, where reputation is
more frequently determined by emotional response than by
analysis. She was later surprised, however, by the universality of
her people when the original of Quirke the butcher was incensed by
the treatment afforded him.

The Rising of the Moon, which also centers upon the emotional
Irish reaction to an "heroic" figure, was produced on March 9, 1907.
It tells how the patriot, Hamilton Rowan, disguised as a travelling
singer named Jimmy Walsh, touched the heart of a police sergeant
by singing the ballad from whose title the play takes its name. The
sergeant allows Rowan to escape, forfeiting his chance for reward
money. The waterside setting of the play relates it to the original
ballad, which commemorates the Rising of 1798; for, in the ballad,
the rebels are told to gather " 'In the old spot by the river. . . .' "[12]

The opening of *The Rising* is an excellent example of condensation
and arrangement of details. The scene is the side of a quay in a
seaport town; and the characters include the sergeant; two policemen, X and B; and "A Ragged Man," the escaped Rowan. The
sergeant is placing posters about, the nebulous description of the
wanted man blends with the anonymity of the other actors in the
masque, and the play becomes an Everyman drama. The sergeant's
admiration for the refugee foreshadows his later change of heart:
"Dark hair—dark eyes, smooth face, height five feet five—there's not
much to take hold of in that. . . . They say he's a wonder, that it's he
makes all the plans for the whole organization. . . . He must have
some friends among the gaolers" (59). The play becomes a proof of
the sergeant's thesis, for he himself turns out to be a "friend" among
the gaolers.

Soon after the play begins, the sergeant chases from the scene the
clever, ballad-singing "Jimmy Walsh," but the troubadour tricks the
patrolman into calling him back by suggesting that he knows something about the escaped convict. Walsh frightens the sergeant by
telling him that the fugitive has committed several outrages against
police. When the sergeant summons Walsh, their physical postures
mirror their mental attitudes. Both men sit atop a barrel, which has

been a prop from the start, in order to "see better"; yet the men sit back to back. They begin the metaphoric journey toward communication, however, when they smoke a common pipe.

Walsh's plan to elicit the policeman's aid is working; and, when he chants the song of Poor Old Ireland, he deliberately misses a line so that the sergeant can supply it. Later, as the singer entunes " 'With your pike upon your shoulder,/At the Rising of the Moon' " (65), he hears a whistle from below, confesses his identity, and removes his disguise. The last gesture is an effective contrast to the "masks" of the other characters and to Rowan's assumed identity: only when he is speaking for Ireland is he "real." Rowan struck a true Nationalistic chord in the sergeant, an effect which Sarsfield fails to achieve in *The White Cockade* (1905) when he tries to inspire the cowardly King James. The fugitive Rowan leaps to safety with words that carry a recurrent motif: economic inequity—"Maybe I'll be able to do as much for you when the small rise up and the big fall down . . . when we all change places at the Rising . . . of the Moon" (67). The sergeant concludes the play as he contemplates the hundred pound reward he has lost and turns to the audience to ask if he is as great a fool as he thinks he is.

The tone of *The Rising of the Moon* is augmented by its desolate setting, which encourages introspection; and Lady Gregory's satire against the police state, placed into the speech of the still-devoted sergeant, anticipates the ambiguity of his later emotions. Unfortunately, Nationalists condemned the play, although it censored so strongly foreign domination and financial inequities by supporting the social justice that Lady Gregory advocated from her girlhood: "It's those that are down would be up and those that are up would be down, if it wasn't for us [the police]" (60).

Indeed, both Lady Gregory and Yeats were shocked at the extremes of feeling that the seemingly innocuous play generated. Lady Gregory objects to the emphasis placed upon the play's historicity, which, she felt, robbed the work of its universal significance. She admitted that the plot is set in the time of the Fenian rising in the 1860's; but she maintained that a more important fight occurs in the mind of the sergeant who has divided loyalties: "and so its human side makes it go as well in Oxford or London or Chicago as in Ireland itself."[13] Yeats, writing years later, complained that everyone had forgotten the political circumstances in Ireland that would not permit production of *The Rising of the Moon* for two years: players would not produce it because they felt that it was unpatriotic to admit that a policeman was capable of patriotism. Conservative leaders of the country, however, felt that the sympathetic portrayal of the policeman would slacken opposition to British rule among the masses.

Notwithstanding objections by Nationalists, the play was received with enthusiasm. It was the Castle's turn, however, to complain. The leading Unionist newspaper castigated the Abbey for slandering the king's forces, and Lady Gregory reminds her readers that Dublin Castle rescinded the Abbey's privilege of using cast-off uniforms of policemen. The administration found in *The Rising of the Moon* "some smell of rebellion and has put us under punishment for its sins. . . ."[14] Prohibiting the Abbey to use the costumes was especially severe since all the theaters in Dublin had the right to the tarnished clothing.

The Jackdaw also focusses upon the need of the Irish peasants to follow a hero, even if they must fabricate one out of gossip and innuendo. The play opens in a small general store in Cloon. Mrs. Broderick, its owner, is illiterate and has been relying upon her friend, Mr. Nestor, the unofficial town adviser, to write to her brother, Cooney, a well-off farmer from Limerick, to help her out of debt. She is summoned to court, for there have been no answers to the letters. When Cooney does come to town, he tells Nestor that he wants to assist his sister but that he does not want her to know the origin of the donation lest she use him in the future. Thus the shrewd Cooney is Lady Gregory's answer to the sentimental hero of *Twenty-Five* who gave away money earned in America in order to help his former loved one.

Nestor considers various means of carrying out Cooney's wish: "I was reading on 'Home Chat' about a woman put a note for five pounds into her son's prayer book and he going a voyage. And when he came back and was in the church with her it fell out, he never having turned a leaf of the book at all."[15] The best solution, Nestor finds, involves the fabricating of an imaginary mine owner. This entrepreneur, whom Nestor invents, is forced to live in his South African mine to keep watch on his workers, and even then the task is difficult because the men are so black they can not be identified. As Nestor spins his plot, the workings of his cunning imagination are clearly etched: "He [the mine owner] does be lonesome now and again, and he is longing for a bird to put him in mind of old Ireland . . ."(79).

The type of bird the miner chooses aids Lady Gregory's satiric picture of Ireland's insularity and lack of enlightenment. The imaginary overseer believes that an ordinary bird would die in the darkness in the shafts; and, as Nestor claims, the manager is willing to pay ten pounds for a jackdaw, a bird who is used to living in chimneys. Nestor asserts, "[I]f any birds would bear the confinement it is they that should do it" (79). When Nestor tells Mrs. Broderick that a ten pound note really given her by her brother came from the African miner, word travels quickly; and the villagers, the magistrates, and the jurors all begin to search for jackdaws to sell to the nonexistent purchaser. When this agent cannot be found, the police are summoned to investigate his disappearance.

In the second half of the play, Nestor sends Cooney to an old mill to look for jackdaws; and Mrs. Broderick begins to lose her reputation when she refuses to tell the source of the ten pounds. Later, still unaware of her brother's assistance, she blames him for chasing jackdaws instead of helping her in her troubles. The police appear at the end of the play as buffoons when they desperately try to find the "man" who is supposedly buying jackdaws.

The Jackdaw is one of the best known of Lady Gregory's plays. The work became a favorite at Vassar College and at Smith College, as Lady Gregory discovered on her first trip to America; for, at Smith, the girls had conjugated a verb "to jackdaw" — to bungle things. When the play was staged at the Abbey on February 23, 1907, Holloway spoke of it as a "mad, merry farce."[16] Since *The Playboy* had been presented the previous month, however, the furor it had created among the Dublin populace could not permit a just hearing for *The Jackdaw*.

The play, like *Hyacinth Halvey*, is too long for its slight plot structure; and the ending is inconclusive. But, despite its flaws, *The Jackdaw* contains a number of hilarious events that are also realistic, satiric commentaries about Irish manners; and the first half of the piece is excellent in dialogue and in its characterization of affected Mr. Nestor as the town philosopher who appears as a figure of wit. His wisdom is garnered from readings in "Tit-Bits" and "Home-Chat" that provide him with amazing tales such as the one about the servant girl in Australia who cut off her finger slicing cabbage. Nestor's chief claim to wizardry is his education: "Travelled I did in the army, and attended school and I young, and slept in the one bed with two boys that were learning Greek."[17] Undoubtedly knowing the habits of ancient Greeks in love and in study, Lady Gregory is commenting upon her villagers' veneration of their leaders and patriarchs.

Yet, a vein of seriousness is seen in the mock-heroic elements of Nestor's portrait. His characterization, like his name, is based upon the old orator who kept peace among the Greeks at Troy during the Trojan war. Lady Gregory's Nestor announces that he has been reading about Ulysses, and he later boasts of his own ability to make plans. He is also compared to Finn MacCool, who "chewed his thumb" but who didn't possess Nestor's wisdom, and to Solomon, who kept order among seven hundred wives but couldn't arrange matters as well as Nestor. Lady Gregory is implying that the Irish, more than most people, must have their heroes whether they create them in the guise of Fianna or merely as loquacious pensioners living in a village of Western Ireland.

Another theme of *The Jackdaw* is stated explicitly by the widow Broderick, who is about to appear before the magistrate to answer for her debt of ten pounds: "Sure it's a terrible thing to go in it and to be bound to speak nothing but the truth" (71). The play demonstrates how the Irish often distort the truth by enlarging, for example, a chance comment out of all proportion. Lady Gregory considered *The Jackdaw* a comedy since, as with *Spreading the News*, "character" determined the plot.

The Workhouse Ward, developing the theme of appearance as opposed to reality, was produced on April 20, 1908. It depicts two old paupers who would rather stay together in privation, fighting and arguing constantly, than live separately in comfort. One old man has a chance to leave the charity ward; but, when he learns that his sister will not permit him to take his companion with him, he refuses to budge from the poorhouse and resumes his verbal feud with his friend at the conclusion of the play. Lady Gregory's play opens in the Cloon workhouse with two paupers, Mike McInerney and Michael Miskell, in their beds. It is the feast of St. Colman, but the two old men are too ill to attend mass.

As the oldsters talk, they describe their ailments in language so colorful that it forms Lady Gregory's nearest approach to the living, sensory imagery of Synge's peasants. Michael Miskell asks, "If you have pains within in your inside there is no one can see it or know of it the way they can see my own knees that are swelled up with the rheumatism, and my hands that are twisted in ridges the same as an old cabbage stalk."[18] Citing imaginary grievances from the past, the men accuse each other of stealing; and they charge each other's animals with having destroyed their adjacent properties. Mike says, "They were not quiet, but very ravenous pigs you had that time, as active as a fox they were, killing my young ducks. Once they had blood tasted you couldn't stop them" (98).

As the two men begin to shake their fists and raise a clamor, Mrs. Honor Donohoe, sister of Mike, enters the room. The outspoken Mike remarks that he has not seen Mrs. Donohoe for five years. The frigidity of the sister's later treatment of Mike is cleverly foreshadowed by her cryptic response: "They bade me come up here by the stair. I never was in this place at all" (100). Mrs. Donohoe announces that she wants her brother to live at the farm now that her husband is dead; but, when Mike refuses to be separated from his friend, the possible sentimentality of the decision is balanced against the cold terseness of Mrs. Donohoe. She wants help with the land, but won't take two men; and she is bringing Mike away partially because she feels disgraced by having a brother in a poorhouse. When Mike refuses the offer, Mrs. Donohoe takes back the suit she has brought for what she thought would be his departure with her. The play ends with the two men throwing everything within reach at each other. Their attempt to disguise the emotional impact of the event contrasts with the inability of the passionless Mrs. Donohoe to resuscitate the embers of her repressed personality. The final scene is psychologically plausible, for Mike has just given up an opportunity for material gain.

Lady Gregory's satire proceeds naturally from the lifelong prejudices of the old men, who argue about the respective names and wealth of their families. Lady Gregory felt that she had captured in their dialogue a great deal of Irish character, especially the instinctive ability of the Irish peasant to sense hypocrisy. She was hurt when the Fays, for whom she had written the play, rejected it as being too local.

The Workhouse Ward was originally called *The Poorhouse*, and its scenario came from a visit that Lady Gregory paid to the Gort Workhouse. She wanted to write the play herself but followed the instructions of Yeats, who felt that a play in Gaelic would help the dramatic movement. Lady Gregory "rather sadly" gave her scheme to Douglas Hyde. Later, after the Fays had left the theater, she received Hyde's permission to rewrite *The Poorhouse*. In *Our Irish Theatre*, she explains that her task was a "complete re-writing":[19] in the first play, the two old men who form the center of *The Workhouse Ward* had been talking to an imaginary audience. When Lady Gregory rearranged the play, she did away with the spectators, and the "dialogue became of necessity more closely knit, more direct and personal. . . ."[20] She found the limited number of characters so successful in this play that she tried the experiment in *Grania*, in which only three people appear, and in *The Bogie Men* (1912), with only two. *The Poorhouse* was performed on April 3, 1907; *The Workhouse Ward*, just a little over a year later.

Lady Gregory wanted *The Workhouse Ward* to be read symbolically. To her, the "two scolding paupers are a symbol of ourselves in Ireland . . .",[21] and her comment reminds one of the warring tribes in *The Image* (1909). But, she implies, her purpose is primarily international and universal; and she tells the anecdote of the Rajputs, "that great fighting race," to illustrate the view that " 'it is better to be quarrelling then to be lonesome' " (260). The Rajputs, having been placed under the *Pax Britannica*, took up opium since they could no longer wage war. Connacht, however, "has not yet planted its poppy gardens" (260).

Over ten years after its performance, *The Workhouse Ward* was parodied by the anonymous Sinn Fein allegory, *The Worked-out Ward*.[22] The two old men became two Nationalists, John Dillon and Stephen Gwynn, named Dillonell and Gwynerney. No insult was intended to Lady Gregory in the piece, which was printed by her own publishers. *The Worked-out Ward* is really a tribute to Lady Gregory's understanding of Irish national character.

The genesis of *The Travelling Man* (1910), a less effective study of Irish rural personality, is found in the legend that is recounted by an old woman who lived in a cabin by a bog road on Slieve Echtge that is about a poor girl whom Christ met on the road and directed to go to the home of a man holding a wake for his wife. The girl worked hard for the widower, proved her loyalty, and eventually married the gentleman. One day, when she was sitting by the door working with a bag of wheat, the Savior asked her for food; but, not recognizing Him, she gave Him only potatoes. When she saw her mistake, she ran after Him and was reprimanded. A broader source for the play is "an Irish belief that Christ himself might be in the person of any tramp of the roads. . . ."[23]

In *The Travelling Man*, Lady Gregory unfortunately omits the salty counterquestioning of Christ by the girl: " 'But why didn't you give me a heart that would like to divide it [the wheat]?' "[24] And the pietistic play illustrates that Yeats's influence on Lady Gregory could be deleterious. The idea for the play was Lady Gregory's, although she and Yeats wrote it together. Later, Yeats wrote a variant of it as a "Pagan play,"[25] *The Black Horse*, which failed to please him; and he abandoned it to Lady Gregory, who "worked it out in [her] own way."

The Gaol Gate (1906), Lady Gregory's coda to *Seven Short Plays*, begins at dawn with Mary Cahel and her daughter-in-law, Mary Cushin, waiting in front of Galway Gaol. It is indeed a "dawn" for the young man, Mrs. Cahel's son Denis, who, unknown to the women, has been hanged. The difference between the two women appears at once. Denis's wife sees the darkness of the jail and speaks permissively of her husband's informing: "I never would wonder at all at anything he might be driven to say."[26] But the hardened Mary Cahel answers that good men were jailed before her son who never submitted because of questioning. Although the sergeant had boasted that Denis' confession was influenced by drink, Mary Cushin tries to mitigate the deed by explaining that the entire village knew anyway that "it was Terry that fired the shot" (6). When Mrs. Cahel discovers that her son actually has died a hero, her reaction is chilling: she rejoices that Denis gave his life for a cause and for his friends. His widow laments the injustice of an innocent man's dying for a guilty one; and, in her unreflective love for life and husband, she anticipates the earthy figures of Sean O'Casey's plays. But Mrs. Cahel, who will go about the streets shouting the truth that makes her happy—that her son has sacrificed his life— ends the play with the patriotic lines, "I to stoop on a stick through half a hundred years, I will never be tired with praising! Come hither, Mary Cushin, till we'll shout it through the roads, Denis Cahel died for his neighbour!" (10).

In *The Gaol Gate*, Lady Gregory records the pressures of Denis' community and establishes a mood of desolation. For example, Mrs. Cahel's motivation is contemptibly practical: she is afraid of her neighbors' scorn should it be discovered that her son has informed. Part of the bleakness comes in the timely reference to the cold night in which Denis was taken away and in the gruffness of the gate keeper who laconically tells the women that Denis is dead and buried and that they missed seeing him by a day. And one might see the mourners as the two Marys who stood at the foot of the cross: their man has been crucified by the political idealism of the community. In describing the attitudes of both women, however, Lady Gregory does not judge but rather presents objectively two very different points of view.

The Gaol Gate is Lady Gregory's favorite among the *Seven Short Plays*. Typically, the source for it is an unlikely one; for the inspiration was derived from three unrelated incidents that occurred over a few months. The most important concerns the young carpenter who was rumored to be an informer, but who was later exonerated and became a hero. The three tales blended into one in a flash, and Lady Gregory wrote the play just as quickly—in three days—and never changed a word.

The play depends, however, upon a somewhat improbable condition: Mrs. Cahel has a letter telling her of her son's fate; but, since she is unable to read, she comes to jail ignorant of the facts. (This device is comparable to Mrs. Tarpey's deafness and Mrs. Broderick's illiteracy.) Also, *The Gaol Gate* might profitably be contrasted with *The Rising of the Moon* in which Lady Gregory creates in a few deft strokes the atmosphere that it takes the entire *Gaol Gate* to manufacture. Then too, personality and politics in *The Rising* are presented in a dramatic form by the song of a travelling minstrel, but *The Gaol Gate* is a meditative poem that consists for the most part of a moving but somewhat solipsistic keen. In *The Rising*, character is delineated through action; in *The Gaol Gate*, through rumination and exposition.

The works included in *Seven Short Plays* are written with much more attention to symbolism and structuring motifs than any of Lady Gregory's contemporaries perceived, for these plays fulfill E. M. Forster's definition of "expansive" writing: they return more than was paid into them by the reader or by the audience. A device as obvious as Lady Gregory's use of name symbolism points to her desire to state more than the literal words of the play. Hyacinth Halvey suggests Hyacinthus, the beautiful youth loved by Apollo, who killed him by accident. From Hyacinthus' blood sprung flowers whose petals are marked with the Greek words for "alas"; and one is reminded of Halvey's continual lamentations and of his accidental "murder" by a community that adores him. Nestor, in *The Jackdaw*, is an Irish Ulysses whose plans always go astray. The Sinn Fein movement had no trouble detecting the allegory beneath the antics of two irascible old men in *The Workhouse Ward*, but this group seems to have minimized another level of symbolism in the play: Lady Gregory's picture of the feuding North and South of Ireland.

In addition, Lady Gregory's use of disguise in *The Rising of the Moon* is an early application of Yeats's theory of the mask. In "Easter 1916," Yeats praises the commoners of Dublin, who donned a heroic mask for a great cause; and in Lady Gregory's play a sergeant, long mired in materialistic concerns, allows his true, inspired self to emerge. Had he not done so, he might have resembled the jackdaw, building his nest in ashes, away from the sun. *The Gaol Gate*, however, is Lady Gregory's warning to avoid excessive Nationalism; and Denis becomes a sheep sacrificed to the community, just as was Hyacinth Halvey in Lady Gregory's lighter use of Christocentric symbolism.

Lady Gregory, though lightly satirizing the citizens of Cloon, wants her peasants to remain as they are with all their foibles rather than see them changed by the rigid codes of the priests and of the police. The police in Lady Gregory's plays are strongly censured and are usually cast as figures of ridicule, as in *Spreading the News* and in *The Jackdaw*, where they look for nonexistent murder victims. The sergeant in *The Rising of the Moon* becomes human only when he ceases to function as an agent of the Establishment. Lady Gregory's foolish lawmen take their places next to lecturers who insist on improving the moral character of rural classes and beside the parish priests who seem ubiquitous.

While pointing out the faults of her subjects—their gullibility, their gossiping, their trivial lives enlivened by vivid imaginations that can create a hero from nothing—Lady Gregory remains objective. Not until much later in her career was she forced to condemn, when the private fantasies of her citizens became grim political realities, moving far beyond the self-contained and sheltered village of Cloon.

II   New Comedies *(1913)*

Lady Gregory's plays in *New Comedies* continue themes and motifs established in *Seven Short Plays*. The collection, with the exception of *McDonough's Wife* (1912), marks not so much a diminution of Lady Gregory's powers as her inability to add much more original description to Gort (or "Cloon"), a limited area that she had already scrutinized. The five plays in *New Comedies* include *The Bogie Men* (1912), *The Full Moon* and *Coats* (1910), and *Damer's Gold* and *McDonough's Wife* (1912).

Hazard Adams finds, conversely, that *New Comedies* completes the world of Cloon, which, he feels, was only partially constructed in the earlier *Seven Short Plays*. The returning characters "fill out a world possessing a degree of universality. . . . The stage setting for *Hyacinth Halvey* would seem to contain a seed of the subsequent action, as if the action were saying to us that *this* is, in movement, what the picture had meant."[27] Adams explains that Lady Gregory felt "uneasy about Hyacinth Halvey's fate," and he cites her note to *The Full Moon*: " 'It has sometimes preyed on my mind that Hyacinth Halvey had been left by me in Cloon for his lifetime, bearing the weight of a character that had been put on him by force.' "[28] He adds, "In *The Full Moon*, she contrives his escape."[29] Adams differs with Ernest Boyd, who "disliked the resuscitation of Halvey and the Cloon characters, thinking it an example of poverty of invention," and who judged *The Full Moon* to be " 'utterly devoid of good humor.' "[30] Adams believes that Boyd "mistook serious comic purpose for sourness and did not see that Lady Gregory was filling out a world rather than repeating herself from a grab-bag of tricks."[31]

One major theme in *New Comedies* (and in the later plays) that was introduced by Lady Gregory in *Seven Short Plays* is the Irishman's stress upon "talk," his dire need to communicate his emotions and dreams. Ann Saddlemyer cites this "craving for talk" in *The Bogie Men* in which one lad speaks of his mother's constant references to his cousin: " 'Did she see him?' asks Taig the chimney sweep. 'She did, I suppose, or the thing was near him. She never was tired talking of him.' " And, in this world of Cloon, "the oath, like the curse, carries greater awe than the threat of more conventional slings and arrows, the greatest penalty of all is to be deprived of 'The Talk.' So Red Hanrahan [of *Hanrahan's Oath*, 1918] . . . suffers the double curse of self-imposed dumbness and cannot be released from his oath until rumour confounds itself."[32]

Adams, who agrees that the "theme of words is important," maintains that all "the complexity of the cultural and political life of Ireland required mythmakers to bring it to shape in the imagination, for the words of political rhetoric had hopelessly clouded every issue."[33] He points out, however, that there is a pathetic side to the Irish emphasis on speech, especially when words degenerate into destructive chatter. In Lady Gregory's *The Wrens* (1914), the servant's "faith in them [words] is excessive. But ironically, it is words that will bring down the parliament—words and the chance appearance of two strolling singers."[34]

Lady Gregory chose to open *New Comedies* with *The Bogie Men*, a play that clearly establishes "appearance and reality" as a main theme of the anthology. *The Bogie Men* describes the meeting of two young chimney sweepers in the way station of a main road in Western Ireland. Each sweep is awaiting the arrival of his first cousin, who, in each case, has been held up to him as a model of surpassing virtue and ability. The lads have tried to imitate their cousins' impossible standards and are miserable over their failure to rise to such heights. When the two discover that they themselves are the first cousins, they vow never again to worship fanciful images. Their identity was revealed when they washed the soot from their faces, and now their true personalities begin to emerge.

The play begins as Darby, a sweep, enters a shed near a coach stop to put on a "showy" suit of clothes and as another sweep, Taig, arrives boasting that he is to be taken to the home of his wealthy cousin, Dermot. As the play progresses, the lads' personalities are clearly distinguished. Although Taig seems so sure of himself, it becomes clear that he is boasting in an effort to preserve his own individuality faced with the threat of taking on a new social position.

The Bogie Men is almost perfectly constructed, with its two characters performing skillfully synchronized gestures and movements. The "recognition scene," for example, employs a clever stage trick: the boys change their clothes, and the maneuver demands that they keep their backs to each other. At last, however, Darby's hat falls off, and the true figure emerges. Although the audience guesses early in the play that the two sweeps are really the fictitious cousins, the dialogue is so clever that the ploy becomes acceptable. Often aphorisms save the theme from stagnation. Once Taig avers, "Ah, what's manners but to refuse no man a share of your bite and to keep back your hand from throwing stones?"[35] Again, as the lads share their herring and porter, Taig states, "I'll strive no more to fit myself for high quality relations. I am free from patterns of high up cousins from this out. I'll be a pattern to myself" (118).

And Taig quotes his mother as she used to speak of Dermot: " 'You have no more intellect beside him,' she'd say, 'than a chicken has its head yet in the shell' " (111).

The stimulus for *The Bogie Men* came from a message sent from Dublin to America swearing that *The Playboy of the Western World* had been driven from the stage and from a response from New York averring that Synge's play was " 'dead as a doornail.' " These two communications led Lady Gregory to muse with "renewed delight on our incorrigible genius for myth-making. . . ."[36]

The Full Moon (1910) explores the almost psychotic effects of falsely venerating the leader. It features many characters from Lady Gregory's previous plays: Shawn Early and Bartley Fallon from *Spreading the News*; Mrs. Broderick from *The Jackdaw*; and the Puritanical Miss Joyce, with Peter Tannian and Hyacinth, from *Hyacinth Halvey*. Fallon is still as melancholy as ever, and he appears at the end of the play with a crate over his head to prevent moonbeams from turning him daft. The laconic Tannian becomes bitter in his condemnation of Halvey in *The Full Moon*; and Mrs. Broderick consoles Miss Joyce at the conclusion of the play over the loss of her "intended," Hyacinth, by assuring her that he might well have gone mad had they married and that she is better off without him. The play introduces Cracked Mary, just returned from her seven months sojourn in a madhouse—and she is the only "sane" character in the work.

The Full Moon centers upon the false supposition that Hyacinth Halvey has been bitten by a mad dog, which turns out to be Tannian's pet, a docile animal. The villagers are willing to believe the rumor, and their desire to chain Halvey to prevent him from biting and thus infecting them is analogous to the barbaric treatment rendered to Christy Mahon at the end of *The Playboy of the Western World*. Capitalizing upon the gullibility of his neighbors, Halvey is able to make an honest statement about his real character at the end of the play and then to escape to a nearby fair; and the villagers, it is implied, will obliterate him from their memories with the same facility with which they have venerated him during the year that he has spent among them. Halvey, as well, has learned a lesson; and, aided by an increased awareness of his own capabilities, he forsakes an opportunity to become clerk of the Union in order to get away from the "insane" residents of Cloon. As Halvey states, "It is foolishness kept me in it ever since. It is too big a name was put upon me."[37] And again, ". . . I'd sooner be among a fleet of tinkers, than attending meetings of the Board!" (49).

The Full Moon contains digressions upon the causes and diagnosis of madness and upon conditions in the local asylum. Yet, a measure of unity is gained by references to a character called "his Reverence," who is mentioned both in this play and in *Hyacinth Halvey* but who is never seen. Since the clergyman is expected to arrive at the start of the play and since his train does come at the conclusion, Lady Gregory gains some unity of time. As the pastor returns, Halvey leaves the village to begin a life of freedom.

Cracked Mary is the most intriguing character in the play, and it is unfortunate that Lady Gregory did not permit her to occupy more time on the stage. Mary's description of the madhouse in which she has recently been incarcerated might well apply to Cloon at large because of its propensity for gossip: "What way could you make friends with people would be always talking?" (36). Interesting too is the manner in which Mary patronizes the people of Cloon by augmenting even their apocalyptic description of the mad dog: "[T]hey say he is as big as a calf" (39). Or, "A milch cow, he to grab at her, she's settled. Terrible wicked he is; he's as big as five dogs, and he does be very strong" (39).

Coats (1910), which concerns two newspaper editors, Mineog and Hazel, from the same town, who have very little news to report, examines the deadening results of a lack of social and political commitment. They meet each week to make sure that their papers will present opposing sides of an issue. In the play, their coats are placed on the wrong pegs as they are dining in a restaurant; and each discovers that, because of the paucity of news, the other has written his rival's obituary. After a lengthy squabble, they decide to publish what they have written about each other but to delete their imagined deaths.

The play begins as Mineog, editor of the *Tribune*, meets for dinner at the Royal House Cloonmore with Hazel, editor of the *Champion*. Their coats are mixed up by the waiter, John: "*He drops coats in putting them up. Then notices broken pane in window and picks up the coats hurriedly, putting them on wrong pegs.*"[38] The window can be interpreted allegorically, as can the coats of the two vapid individuals who can as readily change ideas as garments. This opening gesture begins a commentary upon the complacency of the two editors (who usually have no trouble, common pegs that they are, fitting into the proper holes). One states, "There are some people so cantankerous that they will heat themselves in argument as to which side might be right or wrong in a war, or if wars should be in it at all, or hangings" (122).

When the men have the coats sent to them when they become chilly from the broken pane, this action may represent that their closed minds reject the chance for intellectual fresh air. The two demonstrate their insensitive and unreflective natures by musing that there used to be such interesting events as famines to report, but that even these are over now. *Coats* ends with a reconciliation as the two pallid crusaders help each other with their frocks.

Coats makes a profound attempt to state an important theme through symbols and to structure its events upon an explicit philosophical basis. Lady Gregory tells of two surmises that went into the play: one her own and one Nietzsche's datum concerning war. Her own observations led her to believe that the most violent quarrels are reconciled by the ordinary circumstances of life. From Nietzsche, she discovered that " 'A good war justifies every cause.' "[39] Lady Gregory's effort to integrate the two theses in dealing with the rivals in *Coats* leads her to adopt an only partially successful "battle motif" for the play. For example, John states one theme explicitly: "There to be more of battles in the world there would be less of wars."[40] The dramatic tension of *Coats* is weakened, however, when the argument between the men rambles over a number of random points; for the obituary proved to be an ineffective structuring device: a person's life is a vast area.

In *Damer's Gold* (1912), a miser, who resembles the niggardly editors in *Coats*, undergoes a change of heart and decides to spend his money on his nephew, Simon; and the two men leave at the conclusion of the play to bet on horse races. In joining with Simon, Damer prevents his conniving in-laws from taking his wealth and committing him to an asylum. One of these is his sister, Delia, whose insinuating ways Lady Gregory patterns after the biblical Delilah; for Delia wants to spend Damer's money on her grandiose plans.

Damer's Gold begins with a reference to Damer's almost full gallon jug of gold; and, soon after, the audience discovers that Damer's nephew has one gold piece to his name, just enough to fill the jar and to keep it from jingling. Delia enters Damer's house, along with her husband and Damer's brother. Unknown to the three, the hidden Damer overhears their discussion about his parsimoniousness; and, when he reveals himself, he countermands their efforts to improve the living conditions of his house. He complains that his visitors have removed spider webs: "What call had you to do away with them, and they belonging to myself? Is it to bleed to death I should and I to get a tip of a billhook or a slasher?"[41] He objects to wet turf being put near the fire: "To dry it is it. . . . And what length would it be without being burned and consumed and it not to be wet putting it on?" (139).

Act Two begins with Damer's change of heart: he is now both the charitable Christian and the *bon vivant*. His relatives, thinking he is mad, discuss at length who should receive his money. Here Lady Gregory expertly employs the "simple" Simon's purported feeblemindedness: although he was present during the discussion by the three in Act One, he does not think to tell them that Damer is now "broke," that he has won Damer's money playing cards. When Damer discovers that Simon is his nephew, his old spirit is revived since he sees the lad as having a spark of his own past enthusiasm. Damer colorfully recalls the high spots of his youth and finds another bond between the two of them; Simon was born the same year that Damer procured his house: "The same year my luck turned against me, and every horse I would back would get the staggers on the course, or would fail to rise at the leaps. All the strength of fortune went from me at that time, it is into himself it flowed and ran" (155). The two share the spoils and go to the races, leaving behind the bland security symbolized in the former miser's house.

The dénouement effectively defines Delia's attitude toward her failure to coax gold from Damer: she is willing to bring her brother's empty gold jug home with her to trick the neighbors into believing that she is an heiress so that they will advance her credit: "Ah, what's goats and what is guinea-hens? Did ever you see yoked horses in a coach, their skin shining out like shells, rising their steps in tune the same as a patrol of police?" (156). Delia's character is complex: she longs for beautiful things and speaks of lovely white goats that are for sale: "Little collars I was thinking to buckle around their neck the same as a lady's lapdog, and maybe so far as a small clear-sounding bell" (142).

The first section of *Damer's Gold* is the most effective and the most "comic" by Molière's definition of the term, and the influence upon Lady Gregory of Molière's *The Miser* is recognizable. Lady Gregory first brought Moliére to the Abbey when the theater directors decided that comedy was needed, and Molière seemed appropriate. Lady Gregory volunteered to translate the comedies into Kiltartan: "It was a revelation of what can be done in colloquial dialect."[42] As a result, Molière's *The Doctor in Spite of Himself* was presented on April 16, 1906; and two of his other plays, *The Rogueries of Scapin* and *The Miser*, were adapted by Lady Gregory before she felt confident enough to strike out on her own, with her own miser, Damer. With her re-creation of Molière's dialogue in her translations, Lady Gregory bridged to some extent the gap that separates the Irish peasant from the French playwright's middle class figures. Damer is indeed the "eccentric," the one who wanders from the center or mean of behavior. A true "humours" character, he keeps his clock ahead to save candles and lets his firewood stand under a dripping thatch so that it will not burn quickly.

Lady Gregory lends *Damer's Gold* an aura of timelessness by naming the protagonist after the chandler who bought for almost nothing the kegs of gold that the Danes had covered with tallow to disguise them when they were driven out of Ireland. Another source for the play is an anecdote of Montaigne, which Lady Gregory uses to account for the change in her hero: Montaigne's subject gave away his gold to a youth in order to avoid the most ridiculous vice of old age, covetousness.

McDonough's Wife (1912), which resembles *The Gaol Gate* in its ability to invoke hope in the midst of death, is a hymn of praise to the power of music, to the melody of Irish bagpipes. At the conclusion of the play, the hero sounds the pipes to lure celebrating sheep shearers from a fair in order to insure a decent burial for his wife, Catherine. McDonough had returned penniless and had found Catherine dead, her body about to be seized by men from the charity wards. He was met by two Galway crones who showed little sympathy for Catherine's plight but who argued instead that how a person is buried doesn't matter.

The play opens with the two old women speaking of the death of McDonough's wife in her shabby room in Galway. Outside is a fair, and the scene looks backwards to the semi-Edenic setting of *Spreading the News* (1904) and forward to the Bunyan-influenced *Dave* (1927). The men of the village refuse to bury Catherine because they have been unable to trace her family tree. She came as a stranger to town, and she was unwilling to explain herself merely to satisfy the curiosity of her neighbors. Unless McDonough returns before night, Catherine will be buried by the charity men. When the women of the town refuse to help, their motives soon become clear: they are jealous of Catherine and want, in addition, to revenge themselves on McDonough who brought into the village a woman without a clear background: "It is too lofty McDonough was, and too high-minded, bringing in a woman who was maybe no lawful wife, or no honest child itself, but it might be a bychild or a tinker's brat, and he giving out no account of her generations or of her name."[43] The two hags admit that, because of the villagers' recalcitrance, McDonough had better have enough money to pay for mourners. There is no reason to think that he might return empty-handed since he has just been playing the pipes to the sheep shearers at Cregroostha (Lady Gregory's Roxborough).

McDonough's first word after he returns is Catherine's name; and, in subsequent conversation with the evil old women, he discovers that Catherine died giving birth to a premature child. The hags' reaction is callous: "A great loss it to be at the time of the fair, and all the lodgers that would have come into the house" (118). McDonough curses the men who refused to help with the burial; he explains that he has squandered his money on drink, treating vagabonds and tramps of the same type as the townspeople who scorned Catherine; and he condemns the two hags when they tell him that Catherine is gone and not deserving of such commotion: he contrasts their mercenary beginnings in a "trader's town" with his own rustic tradition of music and romantic love rooted in Orpheus.

Before going out to the revellers, McDonough climaxes the play with a moving speech: "But I am of the generations of Orpheus, and have in me the breed of his master! And of Raftery and Carolan and O'Daly and all that made sounds of music from this back to the foundations of the earth. . . . [T]he servant I myself command is the pipes that draws its breath from the four winds. . ." (123). The men are entranced by the song, whose magic has been foreshadowed by earlier references to the magic pipes of McDonough's father; but, when McDonough permits only the sheep shearers to help with the burial, his restriction is a touch of realism that is meant to balance the sentimental stopping, solely at McDonough's command, of the noises of the fair at the end of the play. The piper announces that Catherine's body will be taken the long way to the fair, through territory similar to that which appeared in *The Gaol Gate* and in *The Rising of the Moon*: "By Williamsgate, beside Lynch's gallows, beside the gaol of the hangings, the salmon will make their leap as we pass!" (124).

McDonough's allusion to Orpheus suggests that a chief source for *McDonough's Wife* was the Greek stress upon burial of the dead; certainly, the play shares elements of Sophocles' *Antigone*, and a comparison of the two works might prove fruitful. In addition, McDonough's response to Catherine's death reminds one of the central episode of *Alcestis* of Euripides when the Galway hut becomes a royal feast hall and when the hero turns into a Hercules in his desire to battle death for his wife: "I to have been in it he would not have come under the lintel!" (119). Again, the war against mortality is stated in terms that might have been enunciated by such a hero as Douglas Hyde's Tumaus Cosdello: "Ugly as he [death] is and strong, I would be able for him and would wrestle with him and drag him asunder and put him down! Before I would let him lay his sharp touch on her I would break and would crush his naked ribs, and would burn them to lime and scatter them!" (119). By contrast, McDonough laments his wife's light-footed dancing and her cheerful countenance. He apparently perceives her as one of the Sidhe, possibly one dancing near the mountain of Yeats's poetry, Ben Bulben: "Your steps following quick on one another the same as hard rain on a flagstone!" (119).

Lady Gregory draws a sharp contrast between the two cynical hags, who are concerned only with physical necessities, and McDonough, who, while he may have squandered his money on liquor, places great worth on human dignity and tradition. Lady Gregory bitterly indicts those who lack an historical sense, and in their shortsightedness the two harridans resemble the strolling players of the later play, *The Wrens* (1914), who allow Irish independence to slip away while pursuing their own selfish aims. McDonough's denunciation of the two women is caustic and his insistence upon a wake is uncompromising. The play is free of banter, and its tone is somber.

McDonough's Wife is a haunting play, and in it Lady Gregory succeeds in avoiding morbidity though her theme is stark. No actor plays the part of a corpse on the stage—an event which helped turn newspaper reviewers against Synge—but Lady Gregory's view of the Galway hags is just as bitter as Synge's perceptions of his rustics.

Indeed, by keeping the dead Catherine off the stage, Lady Gregory is able to paint an even more mordant picture of one aspect of "peasant" personality: malice toward the outsider.

Lady Gregory lifts the simple tale of an impoverished piper to mythic proportions as McDonough becomes both Orpheus and Hercules in his battle for independence. Lady Gregory saw the play as a fable meant to disclose "the lasting pride of the artist of all ages. . . ."[44] She composed her story while looking into the dark waves of the Atlantic from the *Cymric* during her voyage to America in September 1911.

CHAPTER 5

Folk-History Plays

I *First Series: Tragedies (1912)*

*I*rish *Folk-History Plays*, published in 1912, includes *Kincora* (1905), *Grania* (1912), and *Dervorgilla* (1907). In the volume, Lady Gregory completes a project shared with Yeats and Synge: the building of a superhero for contemporary Ireland. The plays are a reaction against the restrictive confines of twentieth century English and Irish commercialism and of the middle class and melodramatic plays of Dion Boucicault (1820–1890). These heroic dramas demonstrate a clear break, as well, with Martyn and Moore, who originally planned to bring Ibsen to Ireland.

In Yeats's dramas the hero is often of a traditional epic nature, a preternatural creature taken directly from the sagas—usually from Lady Gregory's arrangement of them. In dramas by Lady Gregory, however, the hero or heroine springs from peasant motivations. Lady Gregory insists upon the power of womanly emotion inherent in rustics, and all three of her heroines bring ruin upon a country when their passions are repressed. Previous commentators about Lady Gregory's tragedies have noted that she "casts women in the pivotal roles" of the three plays whose subject matter stretches "from the time of Finn to the coming of the English. . . ."[1] Just as important, however, is the fact that Lady Gregory's plays are "expressions of a humanized mythology that grew from the life around her, but that gave back something too—the vision of great things happening among a simple and long-oppressed people." Pointing out the "old ironic saying . . . that the Irish were all kings once," Hazard Adams adds that "Lady Gregory's myth tells us the kings were people, and that they had wives." Thus Lady Gregory's "mythological history rips the veil of the high romantic and reveals a dialogue between husband and wife, a hearth and those who keep it or defile it. Her kings and warriors walk our earth. . . ."[2]

In short, Lady Gregory's tragedies, "whether inhabited by kings or peasants, set themselves in a world familiar to or readily imaginable to the inhabitants of, say, County Galway. Even kings and heroes seem conceived as not higher than we, but about the same."[3] And Ann Saddlemyer concurs in Adams' judgment: "One cannot look therefore in these 'folk-history plays' for fidelity to the commonly accepted textbook versions of the battles of Clontarf and the Boyne . . . instead, as her [Lady Gregory's] notes indicate, she turned to 'the book of the people.' "[4]

Kincora (1905) untangles the web of Irish political and familial relationships just before Brian's defeat of the Danes in the Battle of Clontarf (1014) and elucidates the principals' motives. The historical background of Kincora is intricate. Two kings won fame and prominence in battling the Norsemen, Malachi the Great, who became high king of Ireland in 980, and Brian, king of the Province of Munster. Though the two kings had virtually defeated the Danes by the end of the tenth century, they were unable to get along with each other and decided to divide Ireland between them: Malachi took the northern part; Brian, the southern.

As Lady Gregory indicates, this division "gave great offence to the King of Leinster [Maelmora] whose territory lay in the region assigned by Malachi to Brian. . . . Brian and Malachi immediately gathered an army and met and defeated the united armies of the King of Leinster and the Danes in one of the valleys of the Wicklow hill, Glenmama."[5] This defeat of Maelmora takes place between Act I and Act II of *Kincora*. Historically, Brian married Gormleith *after* the battle of Glenmama in order to gain support to secure the position of high king and to obtain Tara. Lady Gregory, however, begins her play with Brian and Gormleith already married in order to make her Lady Macbethlike character the center of the drama. In *Kincora*, then, Lady Gregory succeeds in focussing the action upon two movements: the efforts of Brian to secure peace for all of Ireland and the attempts by Gormleith, his wife, to continue bloody civil strife.

At the start of Lady Gregory's play, Brian compels Malachi, past husband of Gormleith, and Maelmora, her brother, to sign a peace pact. Maelmora demurs, but Brian threatens to invade his territories; and Maelmora acquiesces to the king's demand. The peace treaty is meant to celebrate the wedding of Brian and Gormleith. Brian will rule the South of Ireland and live at Kincora; Malachi, the North, whose seat is Tara of the high kings. The first act ends, though, on an ill omen. Sitric, son of Gormleith and leader of the Danes, refuses to sign the treaty; and, Maelmora, immediately after he has signed, decides to align himself with Sitric, and thus begins war all over again.

After Maelmora and Sitric have been defeated at the Battle of Glenmama, Brian feels that peace has come at last to the country. He asks a travelling beggar woman to carry a valuable ring throughout Ireland. If she finds that there is no fighting in any part of the country, then Brian's dream of peace is indeed a reality. In the meantime, however, Gormleith interjects an element of sedition: she pleads with Malachi, the high king, to spare her brother (Maelmora) and her son (Sitric). Malachi refuses but realizes that he cannot match the military force of Brian, whom Gormleith does persuade to free Maelmora and Sitric: Malachi surrenders his high kingship to Brian.

In the later stages of *Kincora,* a still restless Gormleith tries to infuse fighting spirit into her husband, Brian, who feels that God's holy will has been implemented, that peace has come to Ireland. Gormleith argues that the provinces are still embroiled in war, but the travelling beggar returns just in time to explain that she has found the entire country at peace. In anger, Gormleith signs a pact with the invading Danes but then repents in time to warn Brian of their approach. Her husband ends the play by preparing to meet the Danes at Clontarf. (Historically, the battle proved a glorious victory for the Irish over the invaders, ending forever the power of the Danes in Ireland.)

Act I of the work takes place at Brian's castle in Kincora. Brian has not yet arrived, and Malachi and Maelmora chat in Kiltartan about the ensuing conference: "Brian may be a great man, Maelmora, and he may have earned a great name. But he hadn't a stim of sense, no more than I myself, when it came to the choosing of a wife."[6] Maelmora's answer provides exposition and prepares the audience for his rebellion: "Let you keep in mind now when you speak of Brian's wife, it is of my own sister you are speaking" (49). Of dramatic importance is Maelmora's complaint that Malachi made the mistake of forcing domesticity upon Gormleith; and the motif is revived in Gormleith's later betrayal of Brian, who had "torment[ed] her to attend to the needle" (49).

Brian appears and emphasizes the theme of peace. As the principals leave, however, servants talk among themselves and predict the coming of the crow of battle, the Morrigu, who in her human form occasions warfare and then feasts upon the dead bodies of soldiers. In this instance, Gormleith is the Morrigu: "Believe me there is some mother of mischief does be always at roost overhead in Ireland . . ." (53). When Gormleith finally appears, she is pictured by a startlingly effective image, one that demonstrates her feigned adjustment to the duties of a housewife and the entanglement in which she is about to immesh the central players of the drama: she has been spearing eels and carrying a net.

A quarrel, incited by Gormleith, ensues over which king is to have the best chair and the best cut of meat. Besides providing exposition, the discussion is symbolically rich: "I tell you if it was not for Brian taking the Danes in hand the way he did, it is hares of the wilderness Malachi might be looking for milk from to-morrow morning, instead of from cows!" (57); for the allusion to cows relates the tenth century battling to such mythical skirmishes as the struggle for the Dun Cow, the Bull of Cuailgne, recounted by Lady Gregory in her work with the Irish sagas. The act ends as the quarrelling spreads to the lesser nobles and as Sitric and Maelmora give up their part in the league. Malachi, stating Lady Gregory's point of view, blames Gormleith for the incipient carnage: she has catalyzed ingredients of disaster that had been there for a long time.

In Act II, Lady Gregory expands motifs and intertwines strands of narrative established as central in Act I. The act begins after the fighting at Glenmama in which the traitors Sitric and Maelmora were defeated by Brian and Malachi. The byplay of the servants explains the results of the battle: Maelmora saved his life by hiding in a yew tree during the worst of the combat. Immediately, however, a new and greater problem arises. Brian is urged by Gormleith to take the high kingship from Malachi, although Brian wishes only to establish the thousand year peace in Ireland, the prophecy of Adam's paradise. When the lady beggar appears, the distraught Brian tells her: "Look now at that ring. It is worth great riches. Take it and give me your prayers. Bring me word that a lone woman can walk Ireland carrying a ring like that, and no one troubling her, and I will take it as a sign I am given leave to sit down at the table of the angels" (68). Gormleith chases the woman away, just as she does later at the climax of the play.

Another narrative strand evolves in Gormleith's subtle arguments in favor of ameliorating the punishment about to be visited upon

Sitric and Maelmora. When she breeds animosity by telling Brian to judge the men, she waits dramatically in a darkened corner during the debate and then comes forward at the critical moment to present her argument: Gormleith implies that Malachi, thinking that the people believe that he is weak, is condemning the two to death to retrieve the opinion of the populace by a harsh deed.

Act III, the finest in the play, begins just before the Battle of Clontarf. Here Gormleith becomes even more emphatically the center of the work, characterized as a dreadfully dissatisfied woman. All that Brian wants to do, conversely, is to fast and to pray. But Gormleith says, "Where is the use of gaining power if you go turn from it after to shadows? Heaven may be there as they say, but it is on earth we are living yet" (77). In having Gormleith compel Brian to call his army together with the hope that the assembled troops might revive his fighting spirits, Lady Gregory cleverly uses an aspect of her protagonist's character to provide a fictitious explanation of Brian's ability to survive against the invaders.

Notwithstanding the retinue, however, Gormleith is disappointed by actions of her brother Maelmora; for, just that morning, Maelmora, although a man of noble birth, had helped peasants carry fir trees to the palace in order to stop an incipient argument among workers; for, having happened upon the scene of the altercation, Maelmora had volunteered to perform the task himself. Gormleith refuses to sew a clasp onto Maelmora's cloak because of his lack of pride. Here Lady Gregory explores personal and universal feelings much more successfully than if she had stayed with her sources—in them, the trees were meant for the ordinary tribute to the king; and Maelmora's act was scarcely a gesture of humility.

Meanwhile, Sitric tells Gormleith that he is bringing the Danes to attack Clontarf. Gormleith is horrified, plans to inform Brian, but then gives Sitric the opportunity to escape. As the unfortunate Brian, ignorant of the planned invasion, begins to disband his army, he is reinforced in his design by the reappearance of the beggar, who has walked through all of Ireland and has found no violence. Gormleith, angered when Brian heeds the travelling beggar, is then ordered by the pietistic Brian to repent her warlike impulses.

Shortly after signing a pledge to aid the Danes, Gormleith listens as the changeable Brian speaks of his infinite trust in his wife. She becomes unstrung: "I cannot—, oh, it must be stopped—they must be turned back—it is not too late—help me, Maelmora, Sitric must

do as I bid him. Call him back—go after him, he must obey me . . ."
(89). When Malachi tells Brian of his wife's perfidy, Brian temporarily loses his mind; Gormleith goes off a dishonored queen; and the
old king regains enough composure to call for his sword to do battle
with the Danes.

From the beginning to the end of *Kincora*, Gormleith is characterized as strong, self-willed, clever, and impatient with the life of
the hearth. She is sufficiently intelligent to carry out her ambition:
to live in a state of constant siege. Maelmora avers that Gormleith
will make a fine wife for Brian if he lets her go "her own way . . ."
(49); and, immediately after the comment, her propensity for in-
trigue is demonstrated while all are awaiting the arrival of Sitric.
When she advises the servants to set the best dish for the greatest of
kings, a fight breaks out among the underlings, each of whom jealously defends his master's honor.

Later, Gormleith saves the lives of Maelmora and Sitric by averring to Brian that, because of the breakup of their marriage, Malachi
will be prejudiced in his decree against the two. When this logic
fails to move Brian, Gormleith makes her clever plea to Malachi that
his sentence of doom for the two rebels comes from his fear of his
people's suspicion that he has "gone soft." She maintains that
Malachi is having the two executed solely to demonstrate his ability
to still govern. In the last act of the play, Lady Gregory presents
Gormleith as a woman torn between her love for her country and
her indignation at the religious zealotry that Brian has adopted. She
despises herself for helping the Danes, but she is driven to the deed
by her anger at the ineffectual Brian. The conflict overwhelms her,
and she temporarily loses control of her emotions.

Lady Gregory admits that she followed written history too closely
in writing her first epic drama, but the difficulties under which she
labored were much greater than she realized. First, when compos-
ing *Kincora*, she was accustomed to the looseness of the saga material that she had transliterated; but she appreciated during the writing of the historical play that such drama demands tautness and
tension. Second, she was hampered by the limited size of the stage
and company at the Abbey and was forced to restrict the characters
in *Kincora* to servants and kings. As Lady Gregory states, "The
small size of our stage and our small number of players forced me to
do away with what our people call 'the middling class. . . .' "[7]
Third, she was almost dissuaded from her task by Yeats, who ad-

vised her to give up her desire to "write a tragedy in three acts upon a great personality, Brian the High King,"[8] after she had made several false starts. In *Our Irish Theatre*, Lady Gregory admits that she perhaps should not have written anything other than her short comedies, "but desire for experiment is like fire in the blood, and I had had from the beginning a vision of historical plays being sent by us through all the counties of Ireland."[9] She believes that religion and history are the two avenues that elicit the greatest Irish response.

Kincora reveals many of the flaws and merits of Lady Gregory's early endeavors and is, therefore, an excellent contrast to her later folk history plays. In addition, *Kincora* was popular for nationalistic reasons rather than artistic ones with Dublin theatregoers and helped to attract an audience to the Abbey two years previous to the *Playboy* riots. One old farmer came the distance from Killaloe, near Kincora, to attend the performance. He left chagrined, because, as he put it, " 'Brian ought not to have married that woman [Gormleith], but to have been content with a nice quiet girl from his own district.' "[10]

Lady Gregory had a great deal of interest in the play and "tinkered" with it for over seven years; but, on occasion, she tested the altered version in the Abbey workshop. Her son designed the set, and O'Casey writes that "the king's Great Hall was shown by the hanging of vivid green curtains; there were shields, embossed with designs of gold upon the walls, and heavy mouldings over the doors. For Brian's tent at Clontarf, a great orange curtain filled the background, with figures standing out against it in green, red, and grey."[11] The first version of *Kincora* was given at the Abbey in 1905 and printed by the Abbey Theatre Publications; and the finished version appeared in the 1912 collection of tragedies.

In another play in the collection, *Grania*, Lady Gregory's attempts to cope with the natural repressions caused by her widowhood are presented. Though no critics have so far developed the point, Lady Gregory reveals in "Freudian" images that were possibly evident to her after the play's composition the sexual frustrations of Grania's proposed union with Finn; and the lines and symbols so permeate the play that they might cast light upon her union with Sir William, a subject for a future biographer.

Failure to consider the psychological implications of *Grania* has resulted, however, in criticism that misses the mark and that varies widely in its evaluation of the play. Miss Ellis-Fermor believes that Lady Gregory has replaced the "masterful urgency" of Grania with a superficial portrait of a "bewildered girl overpowered by love and a chivalrous and protecting man. . . ."[12] Apparently ignoring for the moment the British tradition of meditative speech in much of its historical drama, she complains that too often the speakers merely explain themselves in lengthy discourses instead of "revealing themselves and leaving the explanation to others. . . ."[13] As to Miss Ellis-Fermor's first point, Diarmuid's characterization is relatively unsuccessful; but to equate the literary worth of his portrait with Grania's misses the essence of the work. Malone, on the other hand, believes that Lady Gregory reached in *Grania* her "highest achievement in historical tragedy"[14] and that in the play she surpasses Ibsen in his *The Vikings at Helgeland* (1858).

The opening scene of *Grania* is laid in Almhuin, in legendary Ireland; and the beginning sections provide essential exposition. Finn asks Grania, "Who would be welcome if it was not the King of Ireland's daughter, that will be my wife tomorrow?"[15] At once Grania reveals herself as a fearful virgin, a sacrificial bride, as she projects upon the only apparently benign Finn her own desires for the gentleness and nonsexuality of a father. Once, however, she did experience a moment of passion, and she recalls the scene vividly to the deceptively tolerant older man: "They had been hunting—there were a great many strangers. I was bade keep away from the hall. I was looking from a high window—then there was a great outcry in the yard—the hounds were fighting, the hounds the strange men had brought with them. One of them made as if to attack a little dog I owned at the time—I screamed out at the hounds. Then a young man ran out and beat them away, and he held up my little dog to me, laughing, and his cap fell off from his head" (15). The scene foreshadows the return of Diarmuid before the wedding; and Lady Gregory escapes criticism over the ploy by relating elements in the flashback to Grania's past "shyness" and to the motifs of dream, vision, and trance that appear throughout the work.

The opening exchanges between Grania and Finn are followed by a lengthy discussion of the nature of love. Grania reiterates her motives for the wedding; and, as she voices her hope for an eternal union, a loud peal of laughter is heard off stage. Finn's concept of love is stated at the beginning in order to justify the tenacity of his later pursuit of Grania and Diarmuid: "[O]nly the old it [love] goes through and through entirely, because they know all the last honey of the summer time has come to its ferment in their cup. . ." (19).

Grania discovers that Diarmuid, her childhood love, has come to Almhuin. He is exhausted; and, unknown to Grania, Finn takes his watch for him. In a touching scene, which serves also to introduce the important "light" motif and which parallels the penultimate exchange of the play, Finn puts out all the candles. Grania blunders by protesting her love for Diarmuid to the sleeping figure, whom she cannot see in the dark. Finn rashly accuses Diarmuid of instigating the love affair; and Diarmuid leaves his warrior band in order to protect Grania from a wandering, lonely life. Promising Finn that he will respect Grania's chastity, Diarmuid shows the king a "cake of bread" and swears "I will send you its like, white and round and unbroken at every moon of the year, full moon and harvest moon. . ." (22). As long as the cake is intact, so will be Grania's virginity. A stage trick ends the first act as the king falls down in a jealous faint and the two lovers escape.

Act II begins seven years later, and Diarmuid has broken his pact. He was angered by Grania's coquettish exchange of words with the king of Foreign, that mysterious visitant who appeared by the side of a stream. Having received the attention of the two men, Diarmuid's somewhat belatedly, Grania in a very short time wishes to return to civilization: "I would wish my happiness to be seen, and not to be hidden under the branches and twigs of trees" (27). Diarmuid too aids in the breakup of the idyllic union; he begins to long for a return to the Fianna. Both seem fated by their restlessness, though Grania, at this point a thoroughly feminine power, is the driving force behind the maneuver. She wishes to share the happiness that physical release has given her: "[N]ow I am proud and have a right to be proud. And it is hard to nourish pride in a house having two in it only" (28). She adds, "[B]ut it is to thronged places I will go, where it is not through the eyes of wild startled beasts you will be looking at me, but through the eyes of kings' sons. . ." (28)—of ones who will understand why Diarmuid suffered so many troubles.

Complications arise when Diarmuid discovers that Grania had been more aroused than repelled by the king of Foreign's kiss, and Lady Gregory succeeds here in making Grania a complex character. Finn, disguised as a beggar (really a fourth character, although Lady

Gregory boasted of using only three in the play), comes to the door of the lovers' hut and meets Grania. Now Grania becomes as tough-minded in her search for continued happiness as she was when she eloped with Diarmuid at the outset of the play. She happens upon the practical idea of sending the "beggar" back with a whole cake to stall for time and then boasts in physiological language that suggests her lost chastity of the "broken and torn" (31) promise made to Finn. The "beggar" appeals to Diarmuid's patriotism, telling him that men of Foreign have invaded Ireland; and, despite Grania's counsel to wait until he has raised an army, Diarmuid takes a foolhearty step. His anger is fanned by the "beggar's" ridicule: the king of Foreign has made sexual advances to Grania; yet Diarmuid has let him live. Diarmuid rushes out of the hut as Grania at last offers to stay with him in the woods forever. The act ends with Grania's ironic statement, which foreshadows Diarmuid's death in the final act: "It is in at this door he may be coming before the fall of night" (33).

In Act III, which takes place on the afternoon of the same day, Finn comes to the hut dressed for battle; and Grania utters some of the most powerful and personal words to appear in any of Lady Gregory's plays. According to the heroine, Finn's worst deed perpetrated upon the lovers was not his relentless pursuit but the abstinence from sex that he enforced upon them for so long: "But it is the malice you showed, putting a hedge between myself and Diarmuid that I never will forgive, but will keep it against you for ever" (36). And again, "Because if Diarmuid never left his watch upon my threshold, he never came across it, or never gave me the joy and pride of a wife!" (37).

The dying Diarmuid, having been critically wounded by Foreign, is brought before Finn and Grania. In his delirium, he does not know Grania but addresses her as though she were Finn. This scene, which recalls the earlier episode of Grania's mistaking Finn in the dark for Diarmuid, serves as a device for releasing Grania's bitterness toward Diarmuid's distorted idealism. The two men are reunited in their male warrior clan ethic, and Finn joins Diarmuid in repentance. Their close male communication so offends Grania, who has no place in the emotional complex, that she turns against Diarmuid after his death.

The last pages provide a forum for Lady Gregory-Grania's propagandizing, her insistence that Grania has her own life to lead de-

spite Diarmuid's death. Grania says to Finn, "And as for the love I
had for him, it is dead now, and turned to be as cold as the snow is
out beyond the path of the sun" (43). Grania realizes that Diarmuid
may haunt Finn's memories and vows that, when he returns as a
ghost to censure Finn and her, he will find her prepared to ward
him off. Grania's answer to Finn's warning that the men will ridicule
her if she accepts him is an autobiographically telling one: "There is
many a woman lost her lord, and took another, and won great praise
in the latter end, and great honour. And why should I be always a
widow that went so long a maid?" (45). She demands the crown,
reminding Finn that he had offered it many times before; and she
bravely starts to go out of the tent to face the jeers of the soldiers.

Grania's act of self-coronation is one of many important gestures
in the play that point to Lady Gregory's increasing interest in pan-
tomime and its embodiment in "spectacle." The gesture blends with
the recurrent image of fire, which burned brightly even in the
episode with the "beggar," and with such deliberately symbolic gestures as Finn's twice stooping over the body of Diarmuid.

Grania is ridiculed as she goes out, and her return to accept
Finn's help is probably Lady Gregory's admission that Grania is not
entirely a self-contained person. Finn responds to her humility and
accepts her as his wife: "For we three have been these seven years
as if alone in the world; and it was the cruelty and the malice of love
made its sport with us, when we thought it was our own way we
were taking. . ." (46). Grania defies the "strong" men who would
mock a woman and exits with Finn's arm around her as the laughter
of the troops stops.

Lady Gregory made a stringent selection of legendary material for
Grania, and she deftly ignores such matters as whether or not Finn
consented to Diarmuid's death. Her main interest was in explaining
the enigma of the centuries, Grania's final acceptance of Finn; and
she does manage to construct much of the play around this point. In
one sense, *Grania* is a tour de force; for Lady Gregory's use of the
triangle, which necessitated that only three actors appear on the
stage during the entire three acts, indicates her " 'fascination' " with
" 'things difficult.' " As she states, "For the present play I have
taken but enough of the fable on which to set, as on a sod of grass,
the three lovers, one of whom had to die."[16] In this challenging
scheme, the play has, however, its chief weakness; and Yeats's
comment that indeed the three must be loquacious to sustain the

drama—to avoid the tediousness of three people speaking only among themselves—cannot be discarded. Finally, the play is a direct result of Lady Gregory's desire to dramatize familiar legends. Finn was a more popular figure than Cuchulain; and Grania, Lady Gregory found in her folklore explorations, "is often spoken of as belonging to that small race, as if her story had come from a very early time" (285).

In her notes to *Dervorgilla* (1907), which concerns another villainous heroine, Lady Gregory explains that the heroine, daughter of the king of Meath and formerly the wife of O'Rourke, king of Breffny, was carried off "willingly or unwillingly" (289) by Diarmuid MacMurrough, king of Leinster, in 1152. Dervorgilla is known in Ireland as the one responsible for bringing the English into the land for the first time; for O'Rourke and his allies invaded Leinster; and, in the ensuing wars Diarmuid, driven from Ireland, appealed for help to Henry II of England. Diarmuid MacMurrough was given an army commanded by Strongbow, "to whom Diarmuid promised Leinster as reward" (290). This dire event recurs perpetually in Irish memories; Joyce in *Finnegans Wake* (1939) creates his parable of the Mookse and the Gripes around it, though he assigns much of the blame for Ireland's subjugation to Pope Adrian. The English-Irish conflict was much on Lady Gregory's mind, and she states that she composed the play when circumstances had forced the directors to accept an English stage manager for the Abbey—a move she opposed. Yet, as usual, Lady Gregory was more interested in the personal than in the political side of the allegory; and she focusses her attention upon the woman who outlived all four principals and who is said to have died in 1193 at the age of eighty-five at the Abbey of Mellifont near Drogheda.

Lady Gregory's view of history was influenced by legends of her Kiltartan people. From her old cottagers, she had learned that Dervorgilla was redheaded, was always one to bring about a curse on a country, and was never one to require force to lead her from the hearth into marital infidelity. But these same informants had maintained that the event was not too tragic; for another race, like the Spanish, might have done worse to Ireland, and " 'the laws are good enough. . .' " (293).

The play begins outside of the Abbey of Mellifont in the last year of Dervorgilla's life. A description of the repentant old woman is given through Flann and Mona, her two servants; and one wishes that Lady Gregory had employed such minor characters in *Grania* to avoid monotony. Dervorgilla's generosity, mingled with her implied wish to assuage her conscience, is presented at the beginning: "It is royal she is in giving as in race. Look at all the weight of gold the Abbey got from her, and the golden vessels upon the high altar."[17]

A dark note is introduced into the play by the unseen troop of English soldiers that is heard riding toward the abbey; the air of mystery is enhanced by the comment that no one knows Dervorgilla's name or race. A sense of foreboding is effectively established when one of the characters rushes in with a dead crane. Dervorgilla exclaims, "It has brought to my mind other blood that was spilled, and that I, myself, have to answer for" (98). Dervorgilla, in some ways the reverse of Yeats's Countess Cathleen, who gave her life for her villagers, wonders: "But the people, the people; will they ever forgive what I have done!" (99).

A strange agent of punishment, an itinerant singer, is introduced; and one can see a parallel with the crucial happening in *The Rising of the Moon* (whose first performance was also in 1907), in which song released suppressed feelings. His possibly abrupt appearance is said to be "fated," since Dervorgilla lived so long and because the minstrel has been wandering since the English destroyed his home: "Where would I be stopping? This day five year the thatch I was reared under was burned by the Gall, and all I had of kindred scattered" (99). In the meantime, by contrast, a jovial and ingenuous boy named Owen, who does not know Dervorgilla's background, is sporting in athletic contests. He exemplifies the difference between innocence and experience, but he is destined to be initiated soon into the darker secrets of human nature: "I have the prize won! I was best over the leaps. I have taken the sway!" (101).

As Dervorgilla gives prizes to winners of the games, the itinerant balladeer sings about the evils of MacMurrough, despite Dervorgilla's pleas for clemency: "There is no one who might not be freed from blame, if his case and what led to his wrongdoing were put down" (104). The minstrel mitigates the evil of MacMurrough's deed by castigating the evils of women, and the wiles of Dervorgilla are his prime example. Flann becomes disturbed by the minstrel, who is ignorant of Dervorgilla's relationship to MacMurrough; and the singer leaves the abbey. As Dervorgilla gives money to Flann to bribe the minstrel into leaving the territory, a note of fatalism enters the tragedy: "It is of no use, dreams cannot lie, my punishment must come" (107). Dervorgilla, this Irish combination of Madame Ranevsky from Anton Chekhov's *The Cherry Orchard* (1904) and of Grania, pleads for an understanding of her motives for running away: "O'Rourke was a good man, and a brave man, and a kinder man than Diarmuid, but it was with Diarmuid my heart was" (108).

The ending of *Dervorgilla* introduces a "mad scene." Mona, the old servant, becomes deranged by her husband's murder by the English soldiers; and, in exonerating Dervorgilla, she inadvertently reveals the old woman's identity to the group of sporting children. They return the gifts previously donated by Dervorgilla for the winners of the games, approaching her one by one in formal procession. A touch of delicacy is seen in the hesitation of one young girl, Mamie, before she puts down her gift. Then Dervorgilla advises Mamie to do so also so as not to separate herself from her companions. *Dervorgilla*, then, concerns the failing efforts of the heroine to obtain forgiveness for the crime of bringing the British to Ireland.

Dervorgilla's main fault consists of her belief that money can buy salvation. She regards even spiritual realities as cash-dime enterprises, and she states at one point that God will forgive her since she has passed a day and a night of suffering for every day and night of pleasure. Later she assures Mona that many masses will be said for her servant's dead husband, Flann, to compensate for his having died without the ministrations of a priest. Dervorgilla is quick to offer silver to the travelling minstrel when she first sees his impoverished condition; as noted earlier, she later asks Flann to bribe the beggar into leaving the province; and she has been lavish in her donations of gold to the church. When the young people return the prizes at the conclusion, Dervorgilla realizes that money and gifts will not compensate for the havoc that she has unleashed upon her country. Yet, with all her flaws, Dervorgilla is a character with whom the audience can sympathize, since she works with the only means at her disposal: her wealth and her contrition.

The play contains many devices common to classic tragedy, and it successfully implements the three unities: time, place, and action. Dervorgilla dreams that her identity will be disclosed, and her fears are realized. A tragic omen is found in the dead crane, killed by hunters, which drops blood on Dervorgilla's cloak; and, when British soldiers later slay Flann with a bow and arrow, Flann's murder is described by a vivid "messenger's speech." Flann argues that

Dervorgilla is not really guilty of bringing evil to Ireland, that she is a victim of prophecies. The "Songmaker" with a "common voice" suggests a Greek chorus that reflects the view of ordinary people toward Dervorgilla. And Dervorgilla, bowed with sorrow at the conclusion of the play, is better able to assess her crime and to see herself with clarity.

It is no coincidence that *Dervorgilla* was performed at the Abbey less than a year after the *Playboy* riots and six and a half months after the patriotic *The Rising of the Moon*. With her picture of the cut-throat English in *Dervorgilla*, Lady Gregory helped draw back to the theater the crowds lost because of Synge's play.

II *Second Series: Tragic-Comedies (1912)*

Lady Gregory's three folk comedies, *The Canavans* (1906), *The White Cockade* (1905), and *The Deliverer* (1911), form the "second series" of "tragic-comedies." These plays are not so baroque or so ornately finished as the first three, but what they lack in stateliness they gain in a variety of technique. Moreover, the three plays explore Lady Gregory's differing attitudes toward the Irish virtue (or vice) of idealism; and the contrast between the noble Sarsfield of *The White Cockade*, who decides in the teeth of defeat after the Battle of the Boyne (1690) to fight again for Ireland, and the Parnell-like hero of *The Deliverer*, who is rejected by the people and clawed by wild cats, reflects the turmoils of the years between 1906 and 1911. In its powerful description of betrayal, *The Deliverer* resembles *McDonough's Wife*, produced a year later at the Abbey. As Adams perceptively notes, *The Canavans* and *The White Cockade* "are the sort of comedy that rises from oppression. The foolishness, with its pathetic undertones, is spread equally among tyrants and oppressed, and scorn falls most heavily upon puffery and cowardice." Thus Adams feels that the plays are "in a limited sense 'didactic.' "[18]

The Canavans details the antics of three foolish Irishmen living in the days of Queen Elizabeth: Peter Canavan, a miller; Antony, his brother, a deserter from the queen's army; and Captain Headly, who is searching for Antony Canavan. Headly, who is really a cousin of the brothers, has changed his name to attain respectability in the English establishment. The play, taking place while Essex is "havocking the whole of Munster,"[19] begins in a mill room at Scar-tana. The Canavan brothers have a reputation for timidity, which, the villagers maintain, stems from their great-grandfather's mistakenly killing a witch-hare and eating the heart. Nevertheless, the miller Peter Canavan is offered the post of mayor—but he fears to be regarded with contempt as a collaborator by the townspeople since acceptance of the post demands his swearing allegiance to Queen Elizabeth.

Another problem arises as Peter's army deserter brother Antony enters dressed as a peddlar who is selling the types of ruffs the queen wears. The satire upon Elizabeth is frank and even brutal: "Sure they say she has her hair dyed red . . . since she came to the turn of her age. . . . That she may be dancing quadrilles on a red hot floor this day twelve-month, along with her fitting father, Henry the Eighth!" (183). Antony places Peter in a very difficult position: Peter is afraid to hide him in his shop and is too sensitive about public opinion to give him to the authorities. Impersonation is used when the militia comes to search the premises, for Antony is left to face the soldiers as Peter hides under sacks of grain. The ruse is discovered when Headly sticks his sword through the sack while looking for his laced handerchief: Peter cries out in pain.

When Act II begins, Antony and Peter are awaiting execution; and Peter laments the now futile precautions he has taken to insure a long life: "Drinking every night carrots to clear the blood, and knapweed to ease the bones . . . the nightmare charm, the toothache charm, the charm to quell a mad dog" (193–94). Peter wonders if he will be condemned after his death by the sins of his high-living brother since the heads might be mixed up after the execution. Humor of a somber but realistic sort is supplied by the appearance of the washwoman, the Widow Greely, who comes to visit the condemned men in order to console them: "I am sorry indeed we could do nothing. But we will be coming back again to see you hanged" (198).

The escape of the two brothers is effected when Antony, dressed like Queen Elizabeth, appeals to the narcissism of Headly, who fancies himself to be the Apollo of the army. The act ends with a repetition of the movements of Act I, for Antony once again smears powder over his face, and Peter once more hides under cloth. In Act III, which returns to the mill kitchen, Peter, not knowing that the "queen" was really Antony masquerading, describes Elizabeth at length. As Antony hides the costume in the chimney and as Headly, finding the clothing, thinks Peter has killed his queen, Lady Gregory again uses the "false murder" motif that she had also used in *Spreading the News* and in *The Jackdaw*. Gradually, many of the difficulties are unravelled; but, because Peter is still left in the dark, his situation prepares for the clever dénouement.

At the conclusion, Peter accidently fires a shot at the passing Essex, who, thinking the miller is sending a greeting, salutes him. Peter mistakenly believes that Essex is afraid of him and concludes that he himself is the "strongest" one: "Isn't it the fool I was wasting time—wasting the years—looking here and there for the strongest? I give you my word, it was not till this present minute that I knew the strongest to be myself!" (216). The outlandish events of this final act are controlled by the utterances of Widow Greely: "On our way to the Castle to see the hanging we were, and Antony is after telling us there is no hanging at all. I wish I had got word sooner and I would not have put on my Sunday cloak." Or, "A great deception indeed. They say there is nothing so good for the soul as to see any person die hard" (205).

The plot of *The Canavans*, unfolding in three carefully inter-locked movements, follows naturally from the personalities of the three protagonists. Peter wants only to be safe, to follow the strongest person. When his brother Antony impersonates the queen, who makes Peter mayor of his village, he follows "her" loyally. Later, when he thinks that Antony has killed the queen, he switches allegiance to his brother. Antony, a parody of Mark Antony, apparently, left the army when he saw in the cards that his "number" was up. He is as cowardly as his brother, but he is extremely clever in "disguising" his fears. He devises his impersonation of the queen to enable Peter and him to escape from prison after Headly has captured them. Later he stuffs the clothing into the chimney, and Headly thinks that Antony has murdered the queen. Headly's chief hope in life is to serve his monarch, and Antony gives him this chance with his costuming.

Lady Gregory uses disguise and impersonation in the play to satirize the falsities of monarchs and to parody those who sacrifice national conscience for personal security. Peter Canavan is a miller; yet he scarcely provides the bread that the people really need. Lady Gregory denies that her play has any narrow national purpose since the "desire possessing Peter Canavan to be on the safe side" is universal; but, she maintains, the tendency "jumps to light more aggressively" in a country which, "like Ireland, has been tilted between two loyalties through so many generations."[20] *The Canavans* was written in a lighthearted moment, however, and Lady Gregory believed that "[i]t plays merrily, and there are some who like it best of my comedies" (298).

The White Cockade is, however, truly one of Lady Gregory's finest plays; the work is filled with enthusiasm and life and, in its better parts, excels anything that Lady Gregory ever wrote. Her purpose in *The White Cockade* was to give a dramatic portrayal of Ireland's history, but she was not blinded to the difficulties faced by the indomitable Sarsfield, the protagonist, that were caused by the lack of patriotism among late seventeenth century Irishmen. Although her pictures of the timorous King James and of the dedicated spectre, Lady Dereen, who could walk easily into a Jacobean melodrama, are slightly exaggerated, Lady Gregory gives the audience living characters in Mrs. Kelleher and her husband. These two typify the pragmatic peasantry in a country fighting for its freedom; and, interested in their own survival, they foreshadow the workers of Sean O'Casey's plays. In *The White Cockade*, Lady Gregory evidences an astonishing ability to treat objectively all Irish political points of view. The play was presented in 1905, however, before the beginning Abbey dreams were shattered by the unrepentant hostility of the populace toward Synge.

The play opens in an inn kitchen in Duncannon, and attention is called to three props that recur throughout the work: Owen Kelleher *lying on a hearth playing jackstones*. Mrs. Kelleher *rubbing a bit of meat. A barrel beside her*. [21] In the play, the meat, for example, comes to represent the ordinary comforts that the unidealistic commoner relies upon: mere physical, not spiritual, nourishment; the jackstones, the "games" that not only the boy, Owen, plays, but many of the other characters as well; and the barrel, King James' means of escape.

Mrs. Kelleher, who speaks constantly in proverbs, begins the first scene by faulting her son, Owen. Her bantering is interrupted by the entrance of Lady Dereen, who has lost all of her money supporting the cause of Irish Nationalism. Lady Dereen is the dedicated Anglo-Irish noblewoman who is willing to give all for her country's battle against the English: "*Old Lady comes in. Her hand is over her eyes as if half blind. She wears ragged clothes that have once been handsome*" (221). Through dialogue that contrasts Lady Dereen with the practical Mrs. Kelleher, it is revealed that James II of England will soon fight William of Orange: "It is likely he [James] will have sent orders to the French ship, so. It is to take his orders it was here. The dear knows where it might be tomorrow, and the pigs we have killed left on our hands!" (222). Mrs. Kelleher has the attributes of Bertolt Brecht's antiheroine, Mother Courage, when she attempts to thwart Lady Dereen's attempt to draft Owen into fighting for James. Owen is, however, sent to get news about the impending attack.

The portrait of Owen's father, Matt, who has traits of the stage Irishman, complements that of the lad's domesticated mother. Matt Kelleher ends the first act by drinking, on the floor, with newly arrived French soldiers and thereby stirring his patriotism by use of artificial spirits. To those familiar with the antics of Parnell's half-hearted followers after his fall, the message was clear. Old Kelleher is seen in the politicians of Joyce's "Ivy Day in the Committee Room," a short story in *Dubliners* (1914), which satirizes the venality of Parnell's successors in politics.

The first scene of Act II of *The White Cockade* takes place in a woods where Sarsfield is trying to show James, who is only concerned about his safety, the ways to regain lost ground even after the defeat by William at the Battle of the Boyne, which has just occurred. Lady Gregory switches the levels of action from the commoners of Act I to the nobility as the cowardly James states, "I wonder if this wood is quite safe" (228). Now, the French ship, ironically, is to be used for James' inglorious escape. Owen, too, is an unwitting dupe in the debasing spectacle when he says to King James, who is disguised, "If you belong to King James, you would be safe where I come from, and that is the inn at the harbour of Duncannon" (231).

In this scene, the dichotomy of idealism versus realism is expressed through the contrast between the thoroughly pragmatic King James and his noble advisor, Sarsfield. The king's ignobility is seen in that he is not merely disguised physically but is an imposter in every sense. James loses the audience's sympathy altogether when he kicks the ground in vexation and calls Ireland a detestable place. Owen serves the purpose of highlighting the king's escape route, and he also prepares for his own disillusionment which occurs in his return to his games at the play's end. About the French ship Owen states, "[I]t is not long it will be in it. It will be sailing at sunrise. There will be a boat coming from it after midnight, for the meat my mother has them promised" (231).

When Scene II returns to the inn, Matt is drinking again, even though James has lost the battle—and this time Matt is with a Williamite soldier. This man is a curious person of expediency, a bright literary creation by Lady Gregory: "I'd drink to any of them myself, if I had no other way to get it" (237). One remark foreshadows this Williamite's later (temporary) change of heart and allegiance, effected by Sarsfield's stirring speech: "Dutch or Scotch, there's no great difference. If we had a King of our own, that would be another story" (237). The center of Act II is the moving exordium on kingship that is delivered by Sarsfield in an effort to rouse the flagging James after the patriot has stepped between the disguised king and the Williamites' muskets. The speech serves to win the soldiers to the king's side since they mistake Sarsfield for James; but it fails to inspire the king. Sarsfield states, "I am sorry all the men of Ireland are not on the one side" (240). And later, "To have that royal blood coming from far off, from some source so high that, like the water of his palace fountain, it keeps breaking, ever breaking away from the common earth, starting up as if to reach the skies" (241–42).

In Act III, which opens at the pier at Duncannon on the same night, James, dressed like a priest, attempts to convince the Williamites that he is the king. He finishes by merely being mocked by the soldiers (as was Christ by Pilate's men). Trying to avoid going with Sarsfield to continue the war, the king was exposed as he hid in the barrel that had contained Matt Kelleher's red wine. At the conclusion of the play, Owen returns to his games by the hearth and the Williamites to their cynical attitudes about patriotism. Matt is still the stage Irishman, the one who stumbled over the barrel that hid the king and thus revealed James' hiding place to the enemy. Sarsfield, though he feels that James has broken faith with the Irish people, hesitates for only a moment before recommitting himself. In the best tradition of the Irish saga heroes, he asks, "What is holding me. . . . Maybe the call of some old angry father of mine, that fought two thousand years ago for a bad master!" (254).

The Deliverer (1911), making explicit bitterness that was merely implied in *The White Cockade*, traces the infidelity of the mobs who rejected Charles Stewart Parnell, Ireland's "Uncrowned King." In its terse, well-constructed way, this play employs techniques of later dramatic Surrealism and anticipates the contemporary Theater of the Absurd.[22] *The Deliverer* is really an antiplay, and its format is suited to its negative thesis of betrayal by the populace. When the play opens on the steps of a palace (reminiscent of Yeats's setting for *The King's Threshold*) at the Inver of the Nile, Ard, Dan, and Malachi are mixing mortar and hefting stones at the bottom of the symbolic steps. The workers objectify the theme of discontentment with their leader as they grumble over their living conditions—in a blend of biblical language and Kiltartan dialect. One of the men queries: "What call had our old fathers bringing us away out of our own place?"[23] The opening dialogue is spiced with thinly disguised references to "Egyptian" overlords who are easily identifiable as British by the audience. One grievance concerns the "over-government taking the hens off the floor" (257). The king of Foreign is seen to profit through the workers' sweat.

Thus Lady Gregory uses anachronisms liberally. A "curragh" is found in Egypt, for Dan wishes to steer his way back to his own harbor. A girl from "Spain or Armenia" is said to have her hat cocked for the heir to the Egyptian throne, and the starved workers remark that a large feast is being prepared for this young Moses-Parnell, called in the play the "King's Nurseling": "Sure the bacon they have dressed in frying pans, you would smell it through the seven parishes" (259). The Nurseling (Moses) really belongs to the same family tribes as the three men. A stereotyped, whip-cracking steward who appears on the scene also knows the origins of the Nurseling, of which, it seems, only young Moses is ignorant; but this situation is soon remedied when the youth overhears a conversation detailing his Egyptian parentage.

During a quarrel, the Nurseling-Moses strikes and kills the steward; and now, with the responsibility of leading the chosen people out of Egypt-Ireland thrust upon him, the lad Moses, speaking as gratuitously as a commander in the later Irish Citizens Army, is confident of success: "When this moon will be over and the next moon begun, we will be back in the place our fathers owned" (266). (Malachi had voiced his opinion of the youth earlier: "He will win in the end, but he will not pass within the mering of the Land of Promise.") Almost immediately, however, the commoners begin to

have doubts about the enterprise — and about their new leader—
for all they care about is becoming "estated people" (267). Dan's
counterargument contains an implied allusion to Parnell's planning
ability and outlines a basic political and military strategy for
Ireland—or for any small nation: "[W]e to be out of his hand, every
enemy has any complaint against Pharaoh will be on our own side"
(268). The Nurseling's strategy resembles Hamilton Rowan's tactics
more than those of an Egyptian officer: "The lad has the Heads of
Police sent watching higher up the river, putting in their mind that
the place being deserted there will be wild lads spearing the King's
fish" (269).

But opposition to the Nurseling wins. Dan becomes jealous when
his wife praises the youth, and Ard maintains that the Nurseling is
probably nothing but promises. The priest says that the Nurseling is
not religious, at least not "stiff" in his practices: "He to have broke
out of their creed [Parnell was a Protestant], and not to have joined
in our own, he would not be a fitting leader for ourselves" (272).
Ard's wife complains that he is probably unable to recite the cate-
chism. All feel that he has put on poor weeds out of mockery, and
they soon begin to wonder about his origins—perhaps his mother was
not really married since the tale of finding the babe in the reeds does
not ring true. Lady Gregory relates the comments to two aspects of
Parnell's personality: his unwillingness to explain the obvious to
critics and his disdain for the more stubborn of the mob: "I never
heard that lad to have said two words upon a platform" (273).

The conclusion contains the most violent action in all of Lady
Gregory's works, and it mirrors effectively the psychological and
spiritual mutilation of the exposed leader. Malachi tries to defend
the lad, and the Nurseling attempts to break up the ensuing quarrel,
but he is stoned by the others and thrown over the wall of the palace
to Pharaoh's cats. The cats appeared earlier in the play, where their
vicious claws were mentioned, and now Ard's wife believes that
they will eat the Nurseling's face away so that the group cannot be
blamed for the deed. One is reminded of Joyce's picture of Ireland
in *A Portrait of the Artist as a Young Man* (1916) as the old sow that
devours her own farrow.

The ending of the play hints at the Crucifixion, for the words of
Ard's wife suggest those of the once doubting Roman soldier who
testifies to Christ's divinity after His death: "I wish I didn't turn

against him. I am thinking he might be an angel" (277). Malachi's words convey the moral of the fable: "That young man to have read history he would not have come to our help" (277). The Irish, Malachi implies, have always been ungrateful; they often murdered their prophets.

CHAPTER 6

Later Years: Frustrations and Final Achievements

I *The Backgrounds of Frustration*

THE last twenty years of Lady Gregory's life reveal three or four bright spots in an otherwise dark period. The years are marked by the end of the Abbey Theatre as an instrument for poetry; by ruinous wars in Ireland, which led into Nationalism and its suffocating insistence upon the use of Gaelic; by the failure of the Irish to regain from the British the Impressionist paintings that had been bequeathed to Ireland by Hugh Lane, Lady Gregory's nephew, but that had been claimed by England because of a technicality in Lane's will; and by the loss of O'Casey for Ireland because of the rejection of his *The Silver Tassie* (1928) after he had been discovered by Lady Gregory. Lady Gregory deserves praise not only for her endurance, which kept the Abbey alive artistically for as long as it was possible, but also for the important works of her last years, such as the biography of Hugh Lane and several of her later plays. The last years held a few emotional high points such as, for example, Lady Gregory's warm relationship with O'Casey and with Shaw; but the overall picture is bleak and is characterized by dire events: the death of Lady Gregory's only son as he flew as a pilot over Italy in 1914;[1] the burning of Roxborough during the Irish Civil War of the 1920's; and the loss of Coole to the forestry department in 1927.

The start of this final phase came after the American tour of 1911–1912. Yeats urged Lady Gregory to travel abroad with the Abbey troupe partially because he wished to stay at home to develop a last possible outlet for his poetic plays. When she returned, he decided that the effort was futile; and he then turned over the reins of the Abbey to her as he left for England. It is true that, while under Lady Gregory's leadership, the Abbey began between 1912 and 1916 to cater obviously to popular tastes, that for a long time it

116

would have to rely upon touring for its support, and that it was compelled in the future to ask about any new work, "Will it pay?" Nonetheless, the handwriting had been on the wall for some time, and Lady Gregory cannot be blamed for failing to do a job that Yeats judged to be hopeless. The Irish dramatic movement fell inexorably into three phases, from its beginning role as poetic theater, to its middle stress upon folk drama, and to the final stage before its commercialization: the incarnation of Realism and satire. Miss Ellis-Fermor sees in the Irish movement an analogy to the two stages of Jacobean drama: "with high poetic tragedy on the one side and grim analytical social satire on the other."[2]

The Realistic movement began with Synge (ironically, since Synge was opposed to Realism without "beauty") about 1903; and it had been incorporated by 1910 into a separate and powerful segment of the Irish theater. By 1914 such groups as the Cork Realists had taken over the stage, their first important stride having been the production of Lennox Robinson's *The Clancy Name*—his first play—in 1908. Their members included T. C. Murray, St. John G. Ervine, Seumas O'Kelly, Brinsley MacNamara, and O'Casey. Lady Gregory, who disliked Robinson's view of life from the start, considered it morbid; and she would not consent to grant him a seat on the board of directors until she was compelled to do so in 1923. Robinson accounts for the "ugly" school of Cork dramatists suddenly rearing its head when he writes, "We young men, a generation later than Yeats, later than Katherine Tynan, later than Seamus O'Sullivan, didn't see her [Ireland] as a queen . . ."[3]—or as an idealized personification such as Cathleen ni Houlihan.

Lady Gregory was forced to cooperate with the dissidents; for, in the period after 1916, the Abbey almost perished. Although Yeats advertised the sale of the building in 1919, there were no buyers; but, although some melodrama and farce were introduced to "save" the theater, Lady Gregory, working with assistance from Robinson, managed to retain the Abbey. As Gerard Fay admits, they "kept to the objective of running a theatre on lines which any commercial manager would say led straight to bankruptcy."[4] Peter Kavanaugh, who is usually unsympathetic to Lady Gregory, distinguishes her reaction from Yeats's when he had wanted to close the theater in 1919: "Not so, Lady Gregory. Although she was sixty-seven she refused to allow the theatre to close even if she was compelled to manage it herself."[5]

A temporary halt in the economic demise came in March 1919 with the production of MacNamara's first play, *The Rebellion in Ballycullen*, and with the appearance of Lady Gregory's Wonder Plays, which were written as much to escape from the atrocities of the political scene as to breathe life into the Abbey. The plays did spark a temporary flicker in the cast, and Barry Fitzgerald found his first great part in the king of *The Dragon* (1919) in which Maureen Delany played his queen. Malone, in fact, regards *The Golden Apple* (produced in 1920, after having been published in 1916) as the synthesis of Lady Gregory's previous mystical strains; and he finds that the fable is comparable with the fantasies of Sir James Barrie and Maurice Maeterlinck. At one point during the lean years, Lady Gregory complemented the proceeds from her fantasies by taking up the chore she hated so much, lecturing. On May 12, 1921, she gave in Chelsea her lecture "Making a Play" together with a few other writers who were trying to save the Abbey from extinction.

Their efforts failed in the long run, and a step downward was taken in 1924 when the Abbey became a state-subsidized theater. The Irish Free State had come into being late in 1921, and in 1924 Dail Eireann, its parliament, voted the sum of fifteen hundred pounds for the encouragement of drama. The Abbey got the lion's share of the money, but it had to agree that an additional director, nominated by the minister of finance, would be appointed to the theater's board. Dr. George O'Brien, a professor of the national university, was the first to serve in this capacity.

Yeats and Lady Gregory recognized the effects that such a compromise was likely to bring about, but they agreed to it out of desperation. Yeats would have closed the Abbey altogether, but Lady Gregory, perhaps wrongly, persuaded him to accept the government grant. She favored turning the theater over to the state, feeling that she had done her part to provide Ireland with its national theater; but Dail Eireann already had its hands full with the rivalries of the Irish Civil War, which began in 1922, and turned down the offer. Ironically, the Abbey's becoming the first state-subsidized theater in the English-speaking world led directly to its artistic demise just moments before the theater was to "rise" again (temporarily) with O'Casey's *The Shadow of a Gunman* (1923). It should be noted, finally, that the rejection of O'Casey's *The Silver Tassie* in 1928 marked the last point in the downward plunge of the theater and that Yeats's death in 1939 ended its life. Denis Johnston took over in 1931 the form of dramatic construction that O'Casey had bequeathed to him in 1928 when he "turned aside from his pictures of Dublin slum-life to experiment in stylised forms, using English material."[6]

The theatrical deterioration was closely reflected in the political horrors. These began with the Easter Rising, and they have never ended even though Eamon de Valera's followers agreed to the famous "oath" that concluded the Irish Civil War, in 1927, and entered the Dail. The rebellion or Rising was an adaptation of the Cuchulain legends, even though Standish O'Grady, for example, looked upon Cuchulain as a conservative social influence and believed that recitals of their ancestors' deeds served to keep readers within the bounds of established society. To O'Grady, then, Cuchulain was the symbol of aristocratic sophistication and a contrast to the commercialism of Irish and English middle classes in the 1880's.

On the other hand, the revolutionary, Padraic Pearse, saw Cuchulain as the military savior who would defeat the British in a bloody and widesweeping conflagration. Lady Gregory's popularization of the myths had been turned to a purpose that was quite the opposite of her intended one—even though she remained a staunch Republican and looked upon de Valera as the Irish Abraham Lincoln. And the Rising was brought forcibly home to the Abbey's actors and dramatists, some of whom died in the rebellion. In the action, which began on April 25, 1916, both sides of the street in which the Abbey stood were demolished, including the buildings of the Royal Hibernian Academy, while the theater itself remained unharmed.

From 1918 to 1921, the Irish-English fighting was intensified as the Irish populace at last rallied around the rebels of 1916 who had been ruthlessly hanged by General Maxwell following the Rising. The Black-and-Tans, a crew made bitter by its experiences in World War I, were sent by the British to terrorize Ireland in 1920. In the autumn and spring of 1920–1921, a curfew was imposed on Dublin that moved back from midnight to ten o'clock, then to nine o'clock, and finally to eight o'clock. At that point, the Abbey shut its doors.

Much of the brutality of the time is recorded in Lady Gregory's *Journals*, published by Lennox Robinson in 1947. In September 1920, Gort would have been burned down had it not been for three of the Old Guard police who restrained drunken soldiers from Ennistymon. By January 1921, there was no law at all in Galway, and

Lady Gregory hoped that Coole would be confiscated rather than have its woods destroyed by outlaw bands or by maurauders who thought nothing of chopping down trees without permission. This war was a different one from that of the land league days when the Gregorys had come through with no harm being done to Coole because they had always been considered to be "on the side of the people." For Lady Gregory, the Abbey provided little escape from the turmoils, even while it remained open. In an entry of October 1, 1921, Lady Gregory records that she had asked Michael Dolan " '[I]f our new actors were Sinn Fein' and he said, 'Is not everyone Sinn Fein now?' "[7]

The ratification of the treaty between England and Ireland which ended their "war" took place in December 1921; and it stipulated that Ireland should have " 'in the Community of Nations known as the British Commonwealth' the status of a Dominion, under the title the Irish Free State, and subject to an option in the Six Counties of Ulster which had been established in the Government of Ireland Act of 1920, Northern Ireland, to vote themselves into the new State if they so desired."[8] The twenty-six "southern" counties became virtually independent and formed the Free State; but a civil war resulted within six months between Die Hards, who insisted upon sovereignty for all of Ireland, North and South, and those in the South who favored the "Partition," the Free Staters. DeValera shocked the vast majority of Irish, both North and South, by not accepting the oath—the treaty—that would have admitted him and his followers to the Dail; and he remained outside the Irish Free State parliament during six years of bloody fighting.

The civil war succeeded in destroying what was left of the Persse and Gregory fortunes. Roxborough was requisitioned in 1922 simply because Major Persse's name had been pulled from a bag in a lottery, and it was burned by an unruly gang in 1924. On April 30, 1922, Lady Gregory tells how the discouraged George Russell wished to write a play concerning the seven hundred years of Irishmen who had fought to liberate Cathleen ni Houlihan; but he had discovered that she had turned into a " 'fierce vituperative old hag.' "[9] In August 1922, Lady Gregory, in coming to Dublin, discovered that a bomb had been thrown at Free State troops passing near the Abbey on the afternoon of her arrival. By this time, the Abbey was considered by many to be an instrument of Free State propaganda.

In the midst of the civil war, Lady Gregory wrote her Passion play, *The Story Brought by Brigit;* this devotional work was produced at the Abbey in April 1924. The play affords insight into Lady Gregory's mental and spiritual state when she was faced with the carnage of 1923: "My mind and hand still on my play, I keep wondering what Christ would do if He were here now, and it all seems to go back to 'love worketh no ill to his neighbour,' and the forgiveness of your brothers' trespasses."[10]

The early years of "decline" were lightened by Lady Gregory's friendship with Shaw. In 1916, she helped him with the ending of *The House in the Clouds*, a fantasy that later turned into *Heartbreak House*. In 1919, Shaw submitted to her ken a "resurrection" play he had just written; and she found it, she told him, rather monotonous and a too obvious adaption of the Ossianic type of dialogue. She added stage directions, in addition, to *Saint Joan* (1923) to give it more realism. Shaw was acutely aware of Lady Gregory's personal and artistic worth, and in 1923 he paid her what she considered a great compliment: " 'Some writers have a natural gift for writing dialogue and need no training, and the first that come to mind in a literary sense are Molière, Goldsmith, Chesterton, and Lady Gregory.' "[11]

In 1924, Lady Gregory fought one of her last battles against censorship; and, though she lost, she garnered some consolation and a bit more practice for the defense of O'Casey's *The Plough and the Stars* (1926). Lennox Robinson, secretary of the Carnegie Trust Fund, which had been established to assist the Irish library system, submitted for republication his short story, "The Madonna of Slieve Dun"; and his resignation from his position was demanded on the charge of blasphemy. Lady Gregory argued courageously but—as it turned out—ineffectually against Robinson's dismissal in the fashion she had been using for twenty years. Admitting the importance of doing anything possible to continue the fund, she nevertheless stated, " 'But I do not think it is a possible thing to dismiss the Secretary who has helped our work for over nine years so well, and that with a slur on his character.' "[12]

II *The Hugh Lane Controversy*

Another battle occupied Lady Gregory during the last part of her career and gave rise to her excellent biography of her nephew: the controversy over Hugh Lane's donation of thirty-nine French Impressionist paintings to Ireland. The task was close to her heart: she began to keep her *Journals* from the end of 1916 (after Lane had been drowned in the torpedoing of the *Lusitania*) in order to record the tribulations over Lane's pictures. England's refusal to relinquish the paintings is rendered doubly reprehensible by the fact that the English did not really want them.

In an effort to perform one act of justice in the bitter contest over the paintings, Lady Gregory pursued the course of going from one official to the next with a relentlessness that surpassed the energy behind her folklore collecting years before. Lady Leslie provided Robinson with a description of the tireless Lady Gregory: " 'I remember her trudging in the rain in London to come to see me, as she thought that I, being a friend of George Curzon, would be able to persuade him to hand over the Collection to Dublin. Her umbrella dripped all the time on my best Chinese carpet—and George Curzon refused to give up the pictures.' "[13]

Lady Gregory carried out her pursuit of the French Impressionist paintings almost alone since Yeats had lost interest in the matter as early as November 1918, and his enthusiasm revived only sporadically. By 1924, she had determined never to return the thirty-nine pictures to England if they ever again found their way across the channel; and she saw, even in the compromise offer of a perpetual loan by the British, an example of Ireland's slavery to English interests. After a crucial defeat in 1926, she pinpointed her emotions: "One hates one's own bitterness of feeling as much as the injustice itself."[14] Probing her motives and intentions in the analytical fashion that characterizes the best of her work, she writes: "My stars have been bad, this trouble with eyes, and now apparent defeat after the long struggle and in sight of victory. Perhaps I have put too much of my life and energy into this, yet I don't think I have neglected other duties."[15] The two literary products of her labors are *Hugh Lane's Life and Achievement, with Some Account of the Dublin Galleries* (1921) and *A Case for the Return of Hugh Lane's Pictures to Dublin* (1926).

Lady Gregory begins her defense of her nephew's life and personality in *Hugh Lane's Life and Achievement* by supplying "background" material concerning the differing characters of Hugh's parents, which formed that "romantic unhappy marriage, that ill-mated parentage."[16] Lady Gregory's sister, Adelaide, Hugh's mother, was the beauty of the family in her youth; and Lady Gregory sees in her conversion to Evangelism the spoilation of Adelaide's potentialities. In condemnation of the Pauline view of the female, Lady Gregory finds her sister to be an example of the numerous Irish women made unhappy by a male-dominated society: "[I]n those days the submission ordered by St. Paul was a part of religion" (2). Or again, "From that time [Adelaide's religious conversion in her late twenties] she, who had rustled the brightest silks over the largest crinoline, passionately wished to work for the souls and bodies of the poor" (3). Adelaide married a divinity student of Trinity College six years her junior, who had little prospects for solvency. The wedding gave rise to an idea often found in Lady Gregory's writings: "[E]ach of the lovers was less in love with the other than with an illusion, an idea" (4).

From his birth, Hugh Lane was delicately featured, of patrician appearance according to Lady Gregory, and admittedly somewhat dandified. Like Joyce's Stephen Dedalus, however, Hugh cherished his artistic idealism, which, in his case, took the form of his desire to become some day a director of one of the national galleries. His dedication was combined from youth with his cleverness; and, when very young, he learned the art of bidding up a price on a canvas.

Lady Gregory relates how Lane's first attempt to help Dubliners was greeted by the initial appearance of the infamous charge of self-gain that was to mar all his subsequent projects. Hugh proposed that the Royal Hibernian Academy, which was being starved by Parliament, hold a loan exhibition of old masters. A modified plan was carried out in the successful Guidhall Exhibition, and its very success led to the accusation that Hugh profited financially from the deal. On the other hand, Hugh was refused backing by the Protestant ascendancy class because of his suspicious association with the "Nationalists," Lady Gregory and her group. When Hugh applied for the curator post of the Dublin National Museum, he was rejected; and the job given to a "safe" man, to the uncontroversial Colonel Plunkett, the choice of the Irish Establishment.

Hugh introduced the French Impressionists into Ireland; and, as Lady Gregory shows in *Hugh Lane's Life and Achievement*, his failing efforts to convince citizens to accept his gift of thirty-nine paintings filled the remainder of his short life. After the charge of bringing forgeries across from France dissipated, the populace devised more ingenious arguments against the paintings. In 1907, Lane promised to give the pictures to the Municipal Gallery if a suitable building could be found to house them. Sites refused then by the city fathers ranged from a corner of Stephen's Green, Dublin's downtown park, to the eventually proposed gallery to be constructed on a bridge over the Liffey River which runs through downtown Dublin.

Lady Gregory explains that, while she tried to raise money for the needed building from American friends, Dubliners were ridiculing works that they made no attempt to understand. She tells of how one official compared the Impressionist paintings unfavorably with dime portraits that could be purchased at any stationery store. A member of the Dublin Corporation described the half hour spent in the temporary gallery in Harcourt Street as the most dismal of his life. His colleagues agreed with him and considered the paintings a fad and merely a monument to Hugh Lane.

Lane's donation of the paintings was most vehemently attacked by the papers of Michael Murphy, Healy's supporter in his attack on Parnell years before. As Lady Gregory states, one paper repeatedly spoke of her home, "Gort," as "Crot." No wonder that Lady Gregory formed a bleak idea of Irish politics during this time of persecution for Lane: "political Ireland sees the good citizen, but as a man who holds to certain opinions and not as a man of good will" (122). Her idealism would not let her turn the Abbey into a picture palace, for "we are 'image makers,' and must carry out our dreams!" (127). Even the objection by Irish chauvinists to the employment of Sir E. Lutyens as architect for the Lane building because of his non-Irish birth did not still Lady Gregory's determination to add dignity to Ireland with her nephew's pictures.

On October 11, 1913, the exhausted Lane made a new will leaving the pictures to the National Gallery of England; and he admittedly did so for the purpose of teaching Ireland a lesson about "its want of public spirit" (136). Then came the *Lusitania* and Lane's death, a heroic one; for Lane had died helping women and children to safety. Lady Gregory's comparison of Lane to Raftery held true: "Often like our wandering folk-poet, Raftery, he had 'made a wedding of what was no wedding' by his presence and his gaiety and his gifts" (164). The momentary swell of feeling for Lane in Ireland after his death contrasts with the atrocious treatment his pictures were receiving in England.

As Lady Gregory explains, the problem of the bequest seemed to be solved when the "Codicil of Forgiveness" was found in the desk of Hugh Lane's room at the Dublin National Gallery. Lane amended his will to return the paintings to Dublin, but, alas, he had not had the change witnessed! This error made the works the permanent property of the London National Gallery, despite hundreds of protests, demonstrations, and counterarguments that followed over the years. Lane became an Irish hero—for all the wrong reasons—as Ireland railed against the theft by the British. Lady Gregory tenaciously revived methods of gaining information that she had used years before in compiling material for the Irish sagas as she detailed her reception by those from whom she sought help in effecting the return of Lane's pictures: "And when I returned home in the evening I would write down my day's gains, what I had gathered through a memory that had been trained through the much gathering of folk-lore. And this seemed akin to folk-lore, the tradition coming through many memories, and that come together makes a whole" (238).

All of these inquiries are distilled in Lady Gregory's biography of her nephew, a thoroughly fine work in which she succeeds in measured phrases and with sympathy and without rancor in presenting a contemporary knight of the Red Branch in conflict with modern foes.

III *The Finding and Losing of O'Casey*

Lady Gregory, primarily, is responsible for the discovery of Sean O'Casey's genius; and she fought a lonely struggle to have his works accepted. From the initial rejection of *The Crimson in the Tri-colour* (1921) until her opposition to Yeats and Robinson over *The Silver Tassie* (1928), she alone of the Abbey directors seemed to appreciate the poetry behind the grim lives of O'Casey's tenement dwellers. Her break with O'Casey over *The Silver Tassie* was her greatest disappointment in her later years, apart from her inability to secure the Lane pictures for Ireland. Her motives for rejecting the work, which O'Casey considered his finest utterance, were sincere but tragically misdirected; but they contrasted sharply with those of Yeats and Robinson.

Lady Gregory "discovered" O'Casey in November 1921, and her journal entry of November 5 tells of her finding an "interesting play," *The Crimson in the Tri-colour*, written to demonstrate the cleavage between Labour and Sinn Fein.[17] She took the time to write a lengthy note and sent the play to Lennox Robinson, who along with Yeats, rejected it. When she spoke with O'Casey five days later, she explained one reason for the rejection—it might weaken the Sinn Fein position—and O'Casey readily agreed. Of greater importance is Lady Gregory's famous advice to O'Casey that his strong point was characterization, a counsel which O'Casey repeated to many people, including Holloway, to whom he had once confided his earlier wish to be another Shaw and to place ideas and themes above character development. Despite the faults of *The Crimson*, Lady Gregory did want to produce the work, "to pull that play together and put it on to give him experience, but Yeats was down on it."[18]

Lady Gregory salvaged the content of *The Crimson* from almost indecipherable handwriting penned upon stationery that the impoverished O'Casey was forced to "borrow." Her attitude differed markedly from Robinson's careless indifference toward the tenement-dwelling dramatist. In *Inishfallen* (1949), O'Casey tells of a letter from Robinson explaining that, in moving from Clare to Foxrock, he had lost the play and asking if O'Casey would furnish another copy. O'Casey had no duplicate copy and not even the notes to make another. His disappointment was augmented because Lady Gregory had written to Sean praising him for particulars of the work: "that it was evident the author had something in him; that Mrs. Rosebud was a delightful character and Mr. Rosebud a fine foil to her. . . . But it could not be put on till the Revolution was over; and it must be typed by the theatre, for no-one could possibly attempt the reading of such written manuscript a second time."[19]

The controversy over *The Plough and the Stars* (1926) was not so easily resolved, and it ended with O'Casey's permanent self-exile. The campaign against the play, as far as Lady Gregory is concerned, began with the pleas of Michael Dolan, the theater manager, who warned her to have nothing to do with the work. Since the Abbey had gained back some of its lost crowds, though the quality of its dramatic offerings had slipped, Dolan did not want to lose audiences because of the language in *The Plough and the Stars;* and he doubted that the company would consent to act in the play. He was supported by George O'Brien, the only Catholic on the board of directors and the unofficial censor, whose presence was occasioned by the theater's government subsidy. O'Brien wanted the song of the prostitute, Rosie Redmond, cut from the play; for he and several others felt that its inclusion would disgrace the Abbey abroad. Holloway, too, played a reactionary part by pigeonholing all passers-by and by insisting that Ireland never had a streetwalker.

At the directors' meeting held to discuss the fate of *The Plough*, the aging Lady Gregory battled against censorship. She insisted upon being the spokesman for O'Casey and told O'Brien that the government official, Blythe, " 'had made no condition whatever in giving the subsidy and certainly no hint of appointing a censor.' "20 She insisted to O'Brien, as she had done to the lord lieutenant in 1909 in the controversy about Shaw's *Blanco Posnet*, that " 'Our position is clear. If we have to choose between the subsidy and our freedom, it is our freedom we choose.' "21

Lady Gregory's constant defense of *The Plough and the Stars* came mainly from her understanding of what O'Casey was trying to do. She states, "These quarreling, drinking women have tenderness and courage, showing all through, as have the men."22 She also maintained that refugees from the Black-and-Tans had often received food and shelter from Rosie Redmonds. In addition, Lady Gregory was able to see through the motives of the protesters, such as her old nemesis, Yeats's beloved Maud Gonne: "These disturbers were almost all women who have made demonstrations on Poppy Day and at elections and meetings; have made a habit of it, of the excitement."23

Although Lady Gregory succeeded, with the help of Yeats, in convincing some Dubliners of the literary worth of O'Casey's *The Plough and the Stars*, she revealed deep lacunae in her understanding of O'Casey's personality in the matter of *The Silver Tassie* (1928). In fact, the series of mishaps and misjudgments over *The Silver Tassie*, O'Casey's antiwar play, which combines Expressionism with his usual Realism in a study of the effects of war on the impoverished, led to his ultimate break with Lady Gregory and thus his separation from the Abbey "workshop." Lady Gregory erred in criticizing the play so harshly, but she did not suspect the dire consequences that her act would have. The fiasco began with Lady Gregory's receipt of a letter from O'Casey on the last day of February 1928. In it, O'Casey told her that he had just finished writing and typing in his rough style *The Silver Tassie* and that, when he had typed a couple of copies, he would send, in about two weeks, a copy to the Abbey but to no one else, " 'so that I may be able to say that the Abbey Theatre was the first to get my new effort.' "24 He assured her that he felt it to be the best play he had written, for he had put a great deal of time into perfecting the new methods used in one scene of the play, a poetic dramatization in the trenches, for which he had studied plainsong and Gregorian chant. On St. Patrick's Day, March 17, 1928, he send *The Silver Tassie* to the Abbey and the rough copy to Gabriel Fallon; and he appended the same view that " 'I think it is by far the best work I have yet done.' "[25]

When Lady Gregory did not like the work, she was relieved to find that Lennox Robinson concurred in her negative opinion about it: "I absolutely agree with Lennox Robinson's criticism, the beginning fine, the first two acts; then such a falling off, especially in the last, the 'persons' lost in rowdiness."[26] She assured Robinson that he was correct; Robinson thanked her and sent the play to Yeats, who was to read it before Robinson delivered the verdict to O'Casey. Yeats wrote his opinion of the work, and Robinson sent the package to O'Casey. Lady Gregory, alone of the three, was disturbed by the possible effect of the comments on O'Casey's ego. It would be a severe blow, she reasoned, but he would be struck by its honesty and would be grateful. Still, she passed an uneasy evening brooding about the disappointment that Sean would feel.

Lady Gregory's opaqueness in the matter is difficult to understand. Perhaps she felt that the work was not so good as O'Casey's previous plays and, like a mother correcting a lazy son, wished him to bring *The Silver Tassie* up to his true standards. She certainly did not want O'Casey to publish the work before he had seen the directors' notes. In a journal entry of April 22, 1928, she records Sean's note, " 'I am correcting proofs now and it will be published in a few months' time,' " and she adds "[I] don't like to think he may print it without . . . criticism. . . ."[27] She could not have foreseen, moreover, the savagery of both Yeats and Robinson toward O'Casey after he had lost his chief sponsor among the Abbey directors, Lady Gregory. Their anger grew as the debate over *The Silver Tassie* became public, and both refused to have anything to do with the play. On one occasion Lady Gregory asked Robinson and Yeats toward the end of a "run" of a revival of *The Plough and the Stars* whether they might consider producing it. She writes, "Yeats inclined to it, but L.R. said 'No. It is a bad play.' "[28]

The reasons for Yeats's dogmatic rejection of the work are not difficult to understand, and Lady Gregory should have been able to comprehend them. First, Yeats felt that *The Silver Tassie* was overly didactic, that the message was not integrated with the dramatic action. Second, the play, in Yeats's view, did not appear to be spiritually profitable. Third, Yeats reasoned, speciously, that, since O'Casey had never been to war, he could not accurately describe it. All of these arguments are rationalizations; for *The Silver Tassie*, though it is not O'Casey's finest work, was far better than any other play the Abbey was presenting in 1928. Perhaps Yeats's paramount reason for dismissing O'Casey was his belief that the dramatist was becoming too self-important for the Abbey. After all, O'Casey had planned to publish the play before he had seen Yeats's comments, and he had begun negotiations to have the play produced in England before the Abbey rendered its verdict. Shaw correctly lamented the treatment given the play since he saw that *The Silver Tassie* was a way out of the slough of Naturalism in which the Abbey had immersed itself.

O'Casey never forgave Robinson and Yeats for the rejection; and, though he pardoned Lady Gregory for her role in the debacle, he refused to see her again when she wanted to visit him in London in October 1929. Although he later regretted his decision, he wrote at that time: " 'So, knowing how I feel, and guessing what I would say about the many literary and artistic shams squatting in their high places in Dublin, I feel it would be much better to set aside for the present the honour and pleasure of seeing you and talking with you. Affectionately yours, Sean.' "[29]

The sadness of Lady Gregory's break with O'Casey resides in the fact that she had found in her acquaintance with him a warm and deep emotional experience. Whether O'Casey ever reciprocated her feelings is debatable, but about Lady Gregory's feelings there can be no question. In 1926, when she was separated from Sean for a short period, she experienced emotions so deep that they broke down the barrier of distance that dissuaded some associates in the Dublin world from approaching her: "Perhaps some day suddenly a barrier will go down and I will have made a friend. I have felt near it sometimes with Sean O'Casey and miss him this time in Dublin."[30] Even O'Casey's patronizing treatment of Lady Gregory in *Inishfallen* cannot prevent the warmth of her personality from radiating through the pages. The book is filled with anecdotes that reveal the human side of a woman whose level-headed control was at times the only force that saw the Abbey through its worst financial and political days.

Lady Gregory gave the same care to O'Casey's genius that she had to Yeats's. She knew that his sight was bad and constructed a special arrangement of shaving mirrors for him. She realized that O'Casey was not trained in polite ways and without condescension advised him not to worry about table manners. O'Casey, who makes a satiric point out of this kind gesture in his *Inishfallen*, probably had missed her intention.

O'Casey's description of Lady Gregory's greeting to him upon his arrival at Coole is now a legend. O'Casey finds that Lady Gregory's Western Ireland background accounted for her agility: "she showed her Connacht rearing by compelling her seventy-odd years to climb down, like a stiff gazelle, from the high seat of the side-car, running to the threshold of the house, turning, and stretching out her two hands to say, with a beaming smile, One and twenty welcomes, Sean, to the House of Coole."[31] Lady Gregory waited for O'Casey at the platform at Gort, notwithstanding the arthritis that he recognized in her stilted movements. Sean gained a lesson in horticulture from his stay: Lady Gregory taught him to distinguish the oak, by legend the first tree God made, and the beech, the elm, and the copper beech. As to her presentations, O'Casey does not bother to distinguish her beliefs from the superstitions of the cottagers who lived near her.

The worth of *Inishfallen* lies in the anecdotes that record Lady Gregory's personality in postures that no one except Casey perceived. Though, lamentably, O'Casey treated these unguardedly sincere moments superciliously, a clear picture can be gained by a careful sifting of his data. For example, when Lady Gregory was busy with one of her Gort cakes, she whispered to Sean that the treat would probably be without its usual restorative force. A neighbor was "so perished" with the cold that she had poured the brandy out for him and thus could not use it in the cake. The episode of a new petrol lamp helps complete a picture of the aging Lady Gregory: "[A]s soon as she put a light to it, the thing gave out a mighty hiss. . . ." Bluish white flames flew up, and Lady Gregory's little, puckered face "began to send frantic and harmless puffs of air towards the soaring . . . flame. . . ."[32]

IV   *The Final Achievements In Drama*

Lady Gregory's *The Image* was first presented in November 1909 and it was dedicated, she states eleven years later, " 'to my nephews Hugh Lane and John Shawe-Taylor, image makers.' "[33] The work was written after the *Playboy* riots in Dublin in 1907 and before Lady Gregory's trip to America in 1911; and its plot, centering in a prize lost through quarrelling, was based directly upon the beginning of Hugh Lane's difficulties. In 1920, when Lady Gregory decided to reissue *The Image*, its theme seemed even more appropriate after four years of bloody political scrimmaging. The work appeared in 1922, one year after the Lane biography, and it included three other plays: *Hanrahan's Oath* (1918), *Shanwalla* (1915), and *The Wrens* (1914). *The Image* was then dedicated to the memories of Lady Gregory's two image-building nephews.

The most interesting characters in *The Image* are Thomas Coppinger, a stonecutter, and Malachi Naughton, a "Mountainy Man." The work uses effective symbolism, and the "image" motif is skillfully handled from the beginning. Coppinger's wife comments to her monument-building husband: "It is a queer thing you to be content, Thomas Coppinger, and you knocking out a living among the dead."[34] One is reminded of the parentage of Padraic Pearse, the leader of the 1916 Easter Rising, whose father was a gravestone cutter: "[I]t would seem that from the beginning Pearse was surrounded by death and the heroic monuments to death."[35]

Coppinger, who lives on the "Munster side of the headland of Druim-na-Cuan,"[36] is a dreamer who hopes to accomplish some great deed before he dies. Intruding upon Coppinger's vision is Malachi, who has just discovered his "image" written on a board washed up by the ocean: it bears the name Hugh O'Lorrha. A third strand in *The Image* is woven by the announcement of another character, Hosty, that two whales have been driven onto the beach on the Connacht side of the headland: the whales had been fighting. A lengthy debate follows as to how money from the whales' oil should be spent; and the contention centers upon the worth of Munster and Connacht, the rival parties of the empire. The act closes with the principals arguing points that range from whether a statue should be erected (with the profit from the whales) to what material should be used for it; for *The Image* reflects the tediousness of Irish factionalism.

Act II is concerned with making Hugh O'Lorrha—who, of course, does not really exist—the subject for the statue; for then the unknown man would become the embodiment of Malachi's dream which has convinced the oldster that "O'Lorrha" must have performed some heroic deed or deeds. When Daniel O'Connell is rejected as the subject for the proposed statue because he is a Munster man, his dream of Catholic Emancipation has symbolic overtones because the villagers exclude both the man and his platform. In a probable allusion to Parnell, all men vote for O'Lorrha and give a wicked twist to one character's quotation from the witch, Biddy Early: " 'Let ye be at one . . . and ye will rule the world' " (159). Here Irish oneness is simply specious conformity.

In Act III, the men discover that they have only Malachi's wild visions to tell them about the candidate, the fictitious O'Lorrha. To complicate matters, all of Western Ireland is following their lead in venerating Hugh. At this point, some inconsequential byplay takes place as Malachi criticizes the stereotyped pictures sent from Dublin upon which the statue is to be modelled; and the encounter is probably based upon Lane's rejecting the practice of painting portraits from photographs instead of from actual persons. Time is spent, too, in a search through a family ledger to find O'Lorrha's name; but the only such cognomen is that of a baby baptized the previous day—it turns out—in honor of Hugh.

The principals resume their quarrelling but scatter when the band arrives to begin the ceremony to dedicate the statue. Before they leave, Lady Gregory states the theme of the play through the characters—it is best to keep one's heart secret to oneself. The play ends with the news that the Connemara boys have taken all the oil from one whale and that the other has been washed out to sea in the spring tide. One poetically stated judgment about the Irish is typical of the chief merit of the play, its frequently rich language: "It would be seventeen times better for themselves and ourselves, those beasts to have stopped browsing where they were, in their pen that is beneath the green ocean" (176).

Although Lady Gregory considered the work her "chief play,"[37] Yeats never liked *The Image*, and learning of Yeats's opinion shocked her. An instance of both Yeats's continuing hostility toward the play and of Lady Gregory's continuing sense of its importance is his response to her desire to stage it at the Abbey in November 1924: " '*The Image* will cause a drop, but as you and Lennox want it, you may put it on.' "[38]

The other three plays in the volume lack the philosophical underpinning of *The Image*. In *Hanrahan's Oath*, the poet vows that he will not speak for a year and a day; he is under the erroneous notion that his garrulity caused him to inform on his friend, Feeney, who keeps a still. Because of his silence, Hanrahan is mistaken for a holy man and is isolated from the community; and this confusion is the basis of the play's humor. Hanrahan eventually discovers that Feeney has not been convicted, and he places a curse against the woman who gave him the false information. *Hanrahan's Oath* does contain a touch of complex characterization in this scheming female.

Shanwalla, the slightest of the three plays, combines fantasy and realism, but its scenario is fragmented among horse racing, murder, and the visitation of a dead wife to save her accused husband. *The Wrens* concerns Ireland's loss of independence in 1800 when the majority vote is for union with England and is occasioned by a travelling minstrel and his wife—the "wrens," who care only for their own minor problems. The play is a variant of the legend, "For the want of a nail. . . ."

The background of *The Wrens* is the enacting of the Act of Union (1800) which dissolved Ireland's independent parliament and secured the country as part of Britain. In Lady Gregory's play, this defeat for Irish Nationalism is brought about by the one vote of parliamentarian Kirwan whose servant is so embroiled with the antics of two travelling minstrels outside the House of Commons in Ireland that he fails to hear the bell calling for the vote and thus neglects to summon his master for the crucial decision. In *The Wrens,* Lady Gregory examines the common people who influenced and are affected by great historical events. One "wren," William Hevenor, has pledged not to touch a drop of liquor until the bill for the union is rejected by the voters. He is a Unionist, but he feels that his cause is lost. Hevenor's wife, Margy, is opposed to the union; but, at the conclusion of the play, she finds consolation in the fact that at least her husband will not be able to resume his drinking habits.

Lady Gregory's *Three Wonder Plays,* published in 1923 in the midst of the worst days of battle-torn Ireland, includes *The Dragon* (1919), *Aristotle's Bellows* (1921), and *The Jester* (1923), which is a reference to Shaw. The plays are charming fantasy and excellent children's literature; but each of them reflects pain caused Lady Gregory by the English-Irish military conflicts during their creation—pain that slips almost unnoticed from Lady Gregory's pen at the moments of highest humor. *The Dragon* was produced in 1919 and *Aristotle's Bellows* in 1921, over two years before the dramatic poem that recounts the historical sorrows of Ireland, *The*

Old Lady Remembers. The three plays are generally much more effective than two of Lady Gregory's other books for children, *The Kiltartan History Book* (1909) and *The Kiltartan Wonder Book* (1910), both of which overemphasize the naivete of the Irish cottager supposedly exemplified in Mary Sheridan's tales.

The Dragon begins by picturing a henpecked king (acted by Barry Fitzgerald), whose wife is trying to keep him on a diet. A starker note is introduced with the prophecy that the king's daughter is to be devoured by a "scaly Green Dragon that will come from the North of the World."[39] To prevent this dire occurrence, Princess Nuala must be married at once; but she proves to be a strong-willed, fairy tale Grania and, in one instance, pretends madness to ward off an effeminate suitor.

Manus, the hero of *The Dragon*, comes disguised as a cook to assist the king and his daughter; and the evil advisor to the king, after a series of intrigues, proposes to kill the lad by cooking him in an oven. The king is not at all horrified but sleeps through the advisor's recital of his plan. The Princess Nuala, once willing to marry to save her people, dies of a broken heart when she thinks Manus has been killed; but, in storybook fashion, she is brought back to life. In the clever ending of the play, the Dragon from the North undergoes a literal change of heart when Manus tears out the old one and replaces it with a squirrel's. The impersonation motif is used throughout, and Lady Gregory expends great care upon its execution. The play was written in 1917 to escape from the tragic aftermath of the 1916 Easter Rising, and Lady Gregory was happy because she made an Ulsterman—a "Dragon" from the "North"?— laugh until he cried.

Aristotle's Bellows is a fable that centers upon the nasty Conan, a mock-heroic figure based upon his cynical namesake of the Red Branch, who never said a good word about anyone. The Conan of *Aristotle's Bellows* is constantly harping upon the great days of ancient Greece. Two magic cats allow him to find a bellows that can change situations to their opposites at a blast. All blasts of air are wasted on foolishness: the pigeon that belongs to a lazy woman, for instance, is turned into a crow; but she becomes industrious and eager to keep a clean house. Unfortunately, such broad satire is often interlaced with lyrics as serious and as moving as "Johnny, I Hardly Knew You!" If any theme is apparent in the play, it is the role of constancy in human destiny. Conan states, after his good intentions have come to nothing, that "Aristotle said there is nothing at the end but what there used to be at the beginning."[40] And again, "The world is a very good world, the best nearly I ever knew" (300). Lady Gregory frankly admits that the play is an "escape into a world of fantasy," but one built upon the moral that change must be gradual: "The restlessness of the time may have found its way into Conan's mind, or as some critic wrote, 'He thinks of the Bellows as Mr. Wilson thought of the League of Nations. . . .' "[41] She started *Aristotle's Bellows* in the autumn of 1919, put it aside to work on Lane's biography, and completed it after that book was finished.

In *The Jester* (1923), which is set in the enchanted world, the mythical island of Hy Brasil, the kingdom's princes are trained in ivory tower learning until the Jester, really the sea god Manannan in mortal guise, shows the youths that there is more in life than books. The lads change places with visiting Wren Boys kept by an Ogre to steal for him, only to discover at the conclusion that they are lost royal cousins. The Ogre is really an old man with a mask. The Shavian-type Jester speaks the moral of the piece: "If you have the strong wish to make the change you can make it."[42] And later, after revealing his identity: "To the little god of laughter/ I pay my sacrifice!" (208). A touch of social relevance is given to one scene when the princes almost have their thumbs cut off at the order of their old guardian who thinks they are Wren Boys who are trying to steal the Sword of Justice. When the guardian changes roles and becomes a judge, his personality worsens with his new power—a lesson for the times.

In his discussion of the *Three Wonder Plays*, Hazard Adams locates their human touches in the midst of the supernatural: "But too much can be made of philosophical or moral themes in these plays. Indeed, they are most charming for their incidental comedy, which is typically of folk quality." Adams points out the everyday relevance of their characters: "Even kings and queens discourse on common subjects. . . . In *The Dragon*, for example, the king, a compulsive eater, objects to the queen's nagging efforts to make him diet. It appears that she is what we would now call a natural food freak. . . ."[43]

V Dave

Lady Gregory's one act play *Dave*, an impressive combination of Symbolism and Realism, is the author's finest "religious" work. In it she deftly opens a wide artistic gap between the dreamer, Dave,

and his self-seeking peasant overseers whose counterparts are found
in *The Unicorn from the Stars* (1908). The chief weakness of *Dave* is
the hero's too rapid psychological changes, although this technique
of instant insight is becoming more and more acceptable as a convention of contemporary drama. As Miss Ellis-Fermor states, "Her
[Lady Gregory's] graver writing appears in passages of *Dave*, especially in the description of Dave's vision at the end, which . . . is
sound in itself and seems to be what she intended from the first to
reveal."[44]

The cast of the play includes Nicholas O'Cahan and his wife, Kate;
their serving man, Timothy Loughlin, and his niece, Josephine; and
the foundling, Dave. The work begins with Timothy's scolding Dave
to make him bring in turf. While Dave is being unfairly chastized,
Josephine tells of listening to a preacher asking help for famine
victims of Iar Connacht (the play takes place "*A hundred years
ago*").[45] Josephine's concern foreshadows her later transformation,
and Dave also evinces a beginning compassion. Characters are
defined by their attitudes toward the central issue, the famine.
Timothy states, "The right place for them is the poorhouse, that was
built for the like of that class" (350). Josephine's description of the
famine recalls Sir William Gregory's account of his father's death;
for, in *Dave*, the missionary says of the victims: "No one to give
them burial, but a bag made and the body put in it and thrown in a
hole in the wild bog . . . . And . . . 'in Connemara over it is the dogs
bring the bodies out of the houses, and ask no leave!' " (351).
Nicholas, who is reading a book that traces his ancestry to the Battle
of Clontarf (1014), pays no attention to his wife's pleas for the famine
sufferers. Also, his reading relates to the emphasis placed upon
Dave's lack of "ancestors" — he has no known parents and was hired
when he sought work at the Easter fair. Nicholas callously alludes to
Dave as "A lad whose race and kindred no one knows. . ." (354).

After Nicholas and Kate leave on a brief trip to town, Nicholas is
soundly ridiculed by the two servants. They kick his book, and
Timothy reveals feelings that he keeps carefully hidden when the
master is around: "Himself and his ancient generations! And looking
at myself over the top of it as if I was dirt!" (356–57). The shift of
Timothy from obsequiousness to belligerence is startlingly effective.
When the two servants discover that Nicholas has left the keys to his
money chest, they begin to rob him. Dave, with his basic sincerity,
chides them for the act; Timothy strikes him over the head, accuses

him of drunkenness when the owners return, and then ties the boy while he goes for the police.

When Dave is in his most perilous straits, Kate frees him because of her sudden human experience, a burst of charitable emotion: "The poor child, all of them telling him he was bad, what way could he believe there was the breath of God in him. . . . He is as lonesome as a weaned lamb gone astray among the stones" (362). Kate stresses that no one is sent into the world without a spark of divine love, and her view of Dave is borne out when he begins to feel that salvation is gained by helping others.

Timothy's treachery is exposed; for, when he fails to locate the police, he commits an act of villainy that is reminiscent of Pegeen Mike's treatment of Christy Mahon in the final scenes of Synge's *The Playboy of the Western World*—he tries to put hot tongs on the boy's leg. Josephine recounts Timothy's doings, and he is banished from the house—ironically, not so much for the villainous deed, as for enraging the master by claiming descent from the Danes.

CHAPTER 7

Lady Gregory's Accomplishments: A Summary

THE false image of Lady Gregory's personality and capacities painted by Joyce, Gogarty, and Moore has survived almost to the present day; for even her recent critics have tended to ignore the extent to which her plays, translations, and organizational powers were respected in the early years of the twentieth century. Moreover, what these three satirists left unscathed, the august presence of Yeats tended to obscure. Lady Gregory throughout her lifetime, however, was as much a rebel as any one of her detractors. Her muted but dedicated refusal to accept the status quo began in her desire to break away from the repressive surroundings of Roxborough. In this desire, she was aided by her nurse, Mary Sheridan, who supplied much of the material for her creative works, and by her own ability to select the worthwhile and to omit the dross. Despite her rebelliousness, the physical beauty of her home contributed to her spontaneity and later to her serenity.

A few years later her rebelliousness and her objectivity were evinced by her abandonment of a short-sighted and restrictive Nationalism in favor of a consideration of the individual. Her synthesizing ability resulted in her perception of the magic behind everyday country experiences, in her eye for the key anecdote that reveals the human being behind the political mask, in her surprise with and fulfillment in the resuscitating Gaelic movement, and in her power of remaining distant from the more esoteric philosophizing of Yeats. On a few occasions, Lady Gregory's exuberance led her to judge falsely; but these instances occur primarily in her "wonder works," the magic and fantastic collections which, by implication, she finds equal in importance to the eloquent and noble *Cuchulain of Muirthemne*. In the totality of her work in Irish myth, however, she succeeded in sending Irish culture abroad, even though she paid little attention to historicity.

138

With her liberated personality, Lady Gregory reconciled many opponents at the start of the Irish Theatre movement. She insisted that Ireland have a serious drama; and she was willing during the thirty-three years that followed to take all the steps necessary to promote her ideal. She mollified Edward Martyn during the debate over Yeats's *The Countess Cathleen* (1892), and she later marshalled forces to defend against the mob this "heretical" play, whose heroine sells her soul to the devil to save her villagers from starvation. She opposed censorship of Synge's *The Playboy of the Western World* and of Shaw's *The Shewing-up of Blanco Posnet*. She wore herself out elucidating the meaning of a work to puzzled groups of Irish playgoers. She sacrificed her own creativity by supplying Yeats with dialogue for his early plays, those sometimes awkward combinations of peasant and "poetic" elements. Her task was made infinitely difficult because, since she was politically and religiously in the center, she was mistrusted by Unionists and by Nationalists, by Protestants and by Catholics. All of her work at the Abbey is characterized by her belief that the Irish peasant held the spiritual and emotional key to Ireland's personality, and she therefore made the Abbey in its golden years a peasant theater.

Lady Gregory most probably will be remembered primarily for her briefer works, the *Seven Short Plays* and *New Comedies*. The plays are much more intricate, however, than critics have so far surmised. Lady Gregory's themes explore ordinary cricumstances and foibles of life that are found and depicted in the Cloon types of people. With a deft touch, Lady Gregory prods her characters' propensities for gossip; their stress upon family name; and, in the later works, their emphasis upon a killingly false code of honor. Sometimes the plays depend too much upon "gimmicks," but at their best the structures of the works approach technical perfection, as in *Spreading the News*, *The Rising of the Moon*, and *The Workhouse Ward*. In all three plays, the action rises swiftly to a climax, then proceeds logically to the dénouement, the plot all the time being structured through events that follow naturally from the plays' carefully limned characters. The better plays, generally, are highly condensed, symbolically integrated, and filled with colorful dialogue and rich connotations; while the least important ones partake of an opposing vice, garrulousness.

The longer plays, the folk histories, stem from Lady Gregory's intention of dramatizing and popularizing Ireland's epic figures. The tragedies are eloquent in parts, but they are too often stilted: the virtue of *Kincora* is not its spontaneity, but rather its painstaking elucidation of the heroine's motivations. In *Grania*, however, the author's personal emotions break through the maze of exposition to create a powerful work. Often the tragedies are assisted by Lady Gregory's manipulation of source material and by her keen analysis of the motives that drove historical personages. The folk comedies, such as *The White Cockade*, are unhampered by the elegaic strain and have more "life" in them, though sometimes their comedy, as in *The Canavans*, becomes merely burlesque.

Bringing her artistic talents and her cultural heritage to bear upon the lives and works of Yeats and O'Casey and to a lesser extent upon the work of Synge, who often shared the beauties of her home, Lady Gregory provided much of the dialogue and subject matter for Yeats's Irish plays. Coole, with its rich past, balanced Yeats's view of the chaos of modern life; and its deeply rooted trees appear often in his poetry as symbols of permanence. In addition, Lady Gregory helped to supply Yeats with the Realism that is seen in his finest poetry, such as "Among School Children," "The Tower," and the "Crazy Jane" poems. In the early plays, the combination of Lady Gregory's peasant speech and Yeats's lofty idealism unfortunately produced awkward dialogue and structure, as in *The Unicorn from the Stars* and *The Pot of Broth*. With O'Casey, Lady Gregory saw the Romanticism behind the satire and proved to be sympathetic though, at the last, a misguided friend.

In her final years, Lady Gregory emphasized a strain of mystical thinking that had been present from the start in her works. Its two embodiments, fantasy and spirituality, were objectified by the political horrors of the years after 1916, by her disappointment over the theft of Hugh Lane's pictures, by the growing importance of Realism in the theater, and by the necessity, after so many years, of capitulating to a governmental censor. The fantasies, such as *The Dragon* and *Aristotle's Bellows*, are notable for their blend of burlesque and pathos. The mystical works, especially *Dave*, have their share of literary permanence.

In short, Lady Gregory's career was a rich and full one. She participated in all the central movements of an interesting and vital age, and she shaped the energies of the principals and added her own blend of humor and magic to the more dour moments of Irish Renaissance literary polemics and politics. With a personality that was a combination of deep-rooted tradition and lofty idealism, Lady Gregory seemed to know always just what was needed and how to go about accomplishing her design. At all times, her great wish was to create what was worthwhile and artistically truthful, in spite of nationalistic and religious pressures, and to provide a forum for others capable and willing to add dignity to Ireland.

Notes and References

Chapter One

1. Elizabeth Coxhead, *Lady Gregory, A Literary Portrait*, 2nd ed. (London, 1966); Ann Saddlemyer, *In Defence of Lady Gregory, Playwright* (Dublin, 1966); and Hazard Adams, *Lady Gregory* (Lewisburg, 1973).

2. James Joyce, *Ulysses* (New York, 1961), p. 216.

3. See Edward A. Kopper, Jr., "Lady Gregory and *Finnegans Wake*," *A Wake Newslitter*, new series, IX (December 1972), 103–07.

4. Oliver St. J. Gogarty, *As I Was Going Down Sackville Street* (New York, 1937), p. 294.

5. *Ibid.*, p. 291.

6. *Ibid.*, p. 292.

7. *Ibid.*, p. 291.

8. *Ibid.*

9. Herbert Howarth, *The Irish Writers, 1880–1940* (New York, 1958), p. 84.

10. George Moore, *Hail and Farewell!* (New York, 1925), I, 240.

11. Sean O'Casey, *Inishfallen, Fare Thee Well* (New York, 1949), p. 163.

12. *Ibid.*, p. 265.

13. Ann Saddlemyer, "Image-Maker for Ireland: Augusta, Lady Gregory," in *The World of W. B. Yeats, Essays in Perspective*, ed. Robin Skelton and Ann Saddlemyer (Victoria, 1965), p. 198.

14. W. B. Yeats, *Dramatis Personae*, in *Autobiographies* (London, 1956), p. 391.

15. Sean O'Faoláin, "Fifty Years of Irish Writing," *Studies*, LI (Spring 1962), 93.

16. *Ibid.*, 95.

17. Yeats, p. 392.

18. *Ibid.*, p. 393.

19. O'Casey, p. 178.

20. *The Kiltartan Poetry Book*, pp. 3–4.

21. Howarth, p. 8.

22. "Dedication," *Cuchulain of Muirthemne*, p. vi.

23. *The Kiltartan Poetry Book*, p. 3.

24. *Mr. Gregory's Letter-Box*, p. 206.

25. *The Kiltartan Poetry Book*, p. 4.

26. *Ideals in Ireland*, p. 11.

27. "Notes and Music," *The Comedies*, p. 261. All quotations from Lady Gregory's plays, unless otherwise noted, are from the Coole Edition of her works (New York, 1970). Whenever plausible, page numbers will be included in the text, within parentheses.

28. "Notes and Music," *The Tragedies and Tragic-Comedies*, p. 294.

29. *Spreading the News*, in *The Comedies*, p. 15.

30. Joseph Hone, *W. B. Yeats, 1865–1939*, 2nd ed. (London, 1965), p. 140.

31. *Ibid.*

32. Yeats, p. 395.

33. *Arabi and His Household*, p. 4.

34. *Autobiography of Sir William Gregory*, p. iv.

35. *Ibid.*, p. 140.

36. *Ibid.*, p. 364.

37. *Mr. Gregory's Letter-Box*, p. 2.

38. *Ibid.*, p. 45.

39. *Ibid.*, p. 102.

40. *The Kiltartan Poetry Book*, p. 11.

41. *Ibid.*

42. *Ibid.*, p. 15.

Chapter Two

1. Ann Saddlemyer, "Pan-Celtism in the Nineties," in *The World of W. B. Yeats*, ed. Robin Skelton and Ann Saddlemyer (Victoria, 1965), p. 19.

2. *Poets and Dreamers*, p. 63.

3. *Gods and Fighting Men*, p. ix.

4. Douglas Hyde, *Love Songs of Connacht* (Dublin and Waterford, 1893), p. 3.

5. Ivor Brown, *Shaw in His Time* (London, 1965), p. 18.

6. *Ibid.*

7. Raymond J. Porter, "The Irish Messianic Tradition," *Emory University Quarterly*, XXII (1966), 34.

8. Yeats, p. 455.

9. *Ibid.*, p. 456.

10. *Ibid.*

11. *Our Irish Theatre*, p. 124.

12. "Notes and Music," *The Tragedies and Tragic-Comedies*, p. 303.

13. In *Douglas Hyde*, Gareth W. Dunleavy describes the first meeting of Douglas Hyde and Lady Gregory: "Lady Gregory recalled later that some of her neighbors, wives of the local Anglo-Irish gentry, had sniffed that Hyde

'cannot be a gentlemen if he speaks Irish.' But the gentleman who spoke Irish and translated the *Love Songs* made a great hit with the Lady of Coole." (Lewisburg, 1974), p. 40.

14. *Poets and Dreamers*, p. 47.

15. *The Kiltartan Poetry Book*, pp. 16–17.

16. Hyde, p. 61.

17. W. B. Yeats, *The Celtic Twilight, Men and Women, Dhouls and Faeries* (London, 1893), p. 23.

18. *Ibid.*, p. 18.

19. *Poets and Dreamers*, p. 2.

20. *Ibid.*, p. 22.

21. *Ibid.*, p. 10.

22. *Ibid.*, p. 119.

23. *Ibid.*, pp. 128–29.

24. *Ibid.*, p. 130.

25. A bronze statue of the dying Cuchulain, with the crow of battle on his shoulder, still stands in the General Post Office in Dublin; from this building Padraic Pearse, inspired by his readings in Ireland's mythological past, read the Proclamation of the Irish Republic on Easter Monday 1916.

26. *Cuchulain of Muirthemne*, p. vi.

27. Yeats, *Dramatis Personae*, p. 456.

28. Cornelius Weygandt, *Irish Plays and Playwrights* (Boston and New York, 1913), p. 140.

29. *Ibid.*, p. 141.

30. *Ibid.*, p. 142.

31. Thomas Kinsella, trans., *The Táin* (Dublin, 1969), p. 255.

32. *Ibid.*, p. 261.

33. P. E. More, "The Epic of Ireland," *Shelburne Essays*, first series (New York and London, 1904), p. 152.

34. *Ibid.*

35. *Gods and Fighting Men*, p. 467.

36. *Ibid.*, p. 1.

37. *Ibid.*, p. 436.

Chapter Three

1. Lennox Robinson, *Ireland's Abbey Theatre, A History, 1899–1951* (London, 1951), p. 4.

2. Andrew E. Malone, *The Irish Drama* (New York, 1965), p. 35.

3. Hone, p. 140.

4. *Our Irish Theatre*, p. 6.

5. *Ibid.*, pp. 6–7.

6. Moore, p. 39.

7. *Our Irish Theatre*, pp. 8–9.

8. *Ibid.*, p. 13.

9. Ernest Augustus Boyd, *Ireland's Literary Renaissance* (New York, 1916) p. 307.

10. *Our Irish Theatre*, p. 80.

11. *Joseph Holloway's Abbey Theatre, A Selection from His Unpublished Journal, Impressions of a Dublin Playgoer*, ed. Robert Hogan and Michael J. O'Neill (Carbondale and Edwardsville, Illinois, 1967), p. 62.

12. *Ibid.*

13. *Ibid.*, p. 156.

14. *Our Irish Theatre*, p. 42.

15. *Ibid.*, p. 47.

16. W. B. Yeats, "Estrangement," in *Autobiographies* (London, 1956), p. 482.

17. Yeats, *Dramatis Personae*, p. 416.

18. John M. Synge, *The Playboy of the Western World*, in *The Complete Plays of John M. Synge* (New York, 1960), p. 18.

19. *Ibid.*, p. 19.

20. *Ibid.*, p. 29.

21. *Our Irish Theatre*, p. 116.

22. Una Ellis-Fermor, *The Irish Dramatic Movement*, 2nd. ed. (London, 1954), p. 51.

23. *Our Irish Theatre*, p. 180.

24. *Ibid.*, p. 253.

25. *Ibid.*, p. 193.

26. Ann Saddlemyer, "Foreword," *Translations, Adaptations, Collaborations*, p. x.

27. Hone, p. 143.

28. Daniel J. Murphy, "Yeats and Lady Gregory: A Unique Dramatic Collaboration," *Modern Drama*, VIII (December 1964), 325–26.

29. *Ibid.*, 327.

30. W. B. Yeats, *Cathleen ni Houlihan*, in *The Collected Plays of W. B. Yeats* (New York, 1952), p. 51.

31. Yeats, *Dramatis Personae*, p. 451.

32. W. B. Yeats, *The Pot of Broth*, in *The Collected Plays of W. B. Yeats* (New York, 1052), p. 62.

33. Saddlemyer, "Foreword," *Translations, Adaptations, Collaborations*, p. x.

34. W. G. Fay and Catherine Carswell, *The Fays of the Abbey Theatre, An Autobiographical Record* (New York, 1935), p. 228.

35. Katherine Tynan, *Twenty-Five Years: Reminiscences* (New York, 1913), p. 240.

36. Malone, p. 80.

37. O'Casey, p. 194.

38. Hone, p. 428.

39. *Our Irish Theatre*, p. 140.
40. *Ibid.*, p. 141.
41. *Ibid.*, pp. 141–42.
42. *Ibid.*, p. 147.
43. Hone, p. 239.

Chapter Four

1. "Dedication of the Plays in This Volume," *The Comedies*, p. xviii.
2. *Our Irish Theatre*, p. 90.
3. Ellis-Fermor, p. 75.
4. *Ibid.*, p. 141.
5. *Our Irish Theatre*, p. 91.
6. *Spreading the News*, in *The Comedies*, p. 20.
7. "Notes and Music," *The Comedies*, p. 253.
8. *Spreading the News*, in *The Comedies*, p. 26.
9. "Notes and Music," *The Comedies*, p. 253.
10. *Ibid.*, p. 255.
11. *Hyacinth Halvey*, in *The Comedies*, pp. 34–35.
12. *The Rising of the Moon*, in *The Comedies*, p. 65.
13. *Our Irish Theatre*, p. 96.
14. *Ibid.*
15. *The Jackdaw*, in *The Comedies*, p. 77.
16. Holloway, p. 88.
17. *The Jackdaw*, in *The Comedies*, p. 75.
18. *The Workhouse Ward*, in *The Comedies*, p. 97.
19. *Our Irish Theatre*, p. 90.
20. *Ibid.*
21. "Notes and Music," *The Comedies*, p. 260.
22. Included in *The Comedies*, pp. 299–304.
23. Malone, p. 162.
24. "Notes and Music," *Wonder and Supernatural*, p. 374.
25. *Our Irish Theatre*, p. 105.
26. *The Gaol Gate*, in *The Tragedies and Tragic-Comedies*, p. 5.
27. Adams, p. 73.
28. *Ibid.*, p. 84.
29. *Ibid.*
30. *Ibid.*, p. 85.
31. *Ibid.*
32. Ann Saddlemyer, "Foreword," *The Comedies*, p. ix.
33. Adams, p. 69.
34. *Ibid.*, p. 68.
35. *The Bogie Men*, in *The Comedies*, p. 114.
36. "Notes and Music," *The Comedies*, p. 260.
37. *The Full Moon*, in *Wonder and the Supernatural*, p. 48.

38. *Coats*, in *The Comedies*, p. 121.
39. "Notes and Music," *The Comedies*, p. 261.
40. *Coats*, in *The Comedies*, p. 131.
41. *Damer's Gold*, in *The Comedies*, p. 139.
42. Fay and Carswell, p. 194.
43. *McDonough's Wife*, in *Tragedies and Tragic-Comedies*, p. 116.
44. "Notes and Music," *The Tragedies and Tragic-Comedies*, p. 295.

Chapter Five

1. Adams, p. 64.
2. *Ibid.*
3. *Ibid.*, p. 65.
4. Ann Saddlemyer, "Foreword," *The Tragedies and Tragic-Comedies*, p. vii.
5. "Notes and Music," *The Tragedies and Tragic-Comedies*, p. 287.
6. *Kincora*, in *The Tragedies and Tragic-Comedies*, p. 49.
7. "Notes and Music," *The Tragedies and Tragic-Comedies*, p. 289.
8. *Our Irish Theatre*, p. 92.
9. *Ibid.*, p. 91.
10. "Notes and Music," *The Tragedies and Tragic-Comedies*, p. 288.
11. O'Casey, p. 197.
12. Ellis-Fermor, p. 156.
13. *Ibid.*, p. 160.
14. Malone, p. 160.
15. *Grania*, in *The Tragedies and Tragic-Comedies*, p. 13.
16. "Notes and Music," *The Tragedies and Tragic-Comedies*, p. 283.
17. *Dervorgilla*, in *The Tragedies and Tragic-Comedies*, p. 96.
18. Adams, p. 65.
19. *The Canavans*, in *The Tragedies and Tragic-Comedies*, p. 180.
20. "Notes and Music," *The Tragedies and Tragic-Comedies*, p. 298.
21. *The White Cockade*, in *The Tragedies and Tragic-Comedies*, p. 219.
22. As Malcolm Brown states in *The Politics of Irish Literature* (Seattle, 1972), ". . . *The Deliverer* was the first Abbey play to experiment with the revolutionary new scenery and stage lighting freshly imported from Moscow by Gordon Craig" (379).
23. *The Deliverer*, in *The Tragedies and Tragic-Comedies*, p. 257.

Chapter Six

1. The last part of Lady Gregory's autobiography, *Seventy Years* (1974), details her sorrow over this event. The fact that her son was shot accidentally by friendly ground fire was mercifully kept from her.
2. Ellis-Fermor, p. 8.
3. Robinson, p. 84.

4. Gerard Fay, *The Abbey Theatre, Cradle of Genius* (London, 1958), p. 144.

5. Peter Kavanaugh, *The Story of the Abbey Theatre, from Its Origins in 1899 to the Present* (New York, 1950), p. 114.

6. Ellis-Fermor, p. 201.

7. *Lady Gregory's Journals, 1916–1930*, ed. Lennox Robinson (New York, 1947), p. 160.

8. *Ibid.*, p. 165 (Robinson's note).

9. *Ibid.*, p. 173.

10. *Ibid.*, p. 190.

11. *Ibid.*, p. 213.

12. *Ibid.*, p. 278.

13. *Ibid.*, p. 288.

14. *Ibid.*, p. 310.

15. *Ibid.*, p. 311.

16. *Hugh Lane's Life and Achievement* (London, 1921), p. 1. All further quotations from *Lane's Life* are indicated by page numbers placed in the text in parentheses.

17. *Journals*, p. 67.

18. *Ibid.*, p. 73.

19. O'Casey, pp. 155–56.

20. *Journals*, p. 91.

21. *Ibid.*, p. 87.

22. *Ibid.*, p. 97.

23. *Ibid.*, p. 96.

24. *Ibid.*, p. 104.

25. Gabriel Fallon, *Sean O'Casey, the Man I Knew* (London, 1965), p. 109.

26. *Journals*, p. 104.

27. *Ibid.*, p. 105.

28. *Ibid.*, p. 110.

29. *Ibid*, p. 123. Eileen O'Casey, Sean's wife, writes, "In spite of his affection for Lady Gregory, she had been with Yeats in the refusal of *The Silver Tassie* and the memory rankled." And again, "We could not know that this was the last opportunity we had of seeing Lady Gregory. . . ." See Eileen O'Casey, *Sean* (London, 1973), pp. 82–83.

30. *Journals*, p. 318.

31. S. O'Casey, p. 182.

32. *Ibid.*, p. 185. O'Casey rendered his final verdict on Lady Gregory almost three decades after her death: " '*She* was the genius behind the Abbey, you know. A lot of people think it was Yeats, but it wasn't. . . . But Lady Gregory was the *real* genius. She was a marvellous woman . . . selfless, single-minded. . . . She came of an old, aristocratic, landownin'

family, and she really cared for Ireland and Irish literature and the Gaelic tongue. It was she who found and inspired and encouraged the writers, and told them what to write, and how to write it. It was she made the Abbey what it was. . . ." See *The Sting and the Twinkle*, eds. E. H. Mikhail and John O'Riordan (New York, 1975), p. 112.

33. *The Image*, in *The Image and Other Plays*, p. 3.

34. *The Image*, in *Wonder and Supernatural*, p. 131.

35. William Irwin Thompson, *The Imagination of an Insurrection, Dublin, Easter 1916* (New York, 1967), p. 75.

36. *The Image*, in *Wonder and Supernatural*, p. 133.

37. *Journals*, p. 81.

38. *Ibid.*

39. *The Dragon*, in *Wonder and Supernatural*, p. 218.

40. *Aristotle's Bellows*, in *Wonder and Supernatural*, p. 300.

41. "Notes and Music," *Wonder and Supernatural*, p. 394.

42. *The Jester*, in *Wonder and Supernatural*, p. 182.

43. Adams, p. 94.

44. Ellis-Fermor, p. 151.

45. *Dave*, in *Wonder and Supernatural*, p. 349.

Selected Bibliography

PRIMARY SOURCES

Many of Lady Gregory's works have been reprinted in The Coole Edition (New York: Oxford University Press, 1970). *The Collected Plays*, ed. Ann Saddlemyer, includes Volumes V, VI, VII, and VIII in this Coole Edition (vol. V: *The Comedies of Lady Gregory;* VI: *The Tragedies and Tragic-Comedies of Lady Gregory;* VII: *The Wonder and Supernatural Plays of Lady Gregory;* VIII: *The Translations and Adaptations of Lady Gregory and Her Collaborations with Douglas Hyde and W. B. Yeats*). Given below are other publication data concerning Lady Gregory's principal works, including her plays, which are listed in chronological order of publication.

1. Plays

Seven Short Plays. Dublin: Maunsel and Co., Ltd., 1909. [Includes *Spreading the News, Hyacinth Halvey, The Rising of the Moon, The Jackdaw, The Workhouse Ward, The Travelling Man,* and *The Gaol Gate.*]
The Image. Dublin: Maunsel and Co., Ltd., 1910.
Irish Folk-History Plays. First and second series. New York and London: G. P. Putnam's Sons, 1912. [First series includes the "tragedies": *Kincora, Grania,* and *Dervorgilla;* second series, the "tragic-comedies": *The Canavans, The White Cockade,* and *The Deliverer.*]
New Comedies. New York and London: G. P. Putnam's Sons, 1913. [Includes *The Bogie Men, The Full Moon, Coats, Damer's Gold,* and *McDonough's Wife.*]
The Golden Apple. New York and London: G. P. Putnam's Sons, 1916.
The Image and Other Plays. New York and London: G. P. Putnam's Sons, 1922. [Includes the revised *Image* and three other plays: *Hanrahan's Oath, Shanwalla,* and *The Wrens.*]
Three Wonder Plays. New York and London: G. P. Putnam's Sons, 1923. [Includes *The Dragon, Aristotle's Bellows,* and *The Jester.*]
The Story Brought by Brigid. New York and London: G. P. Putnam's Sons, 1924.
Three Last Plays. New York and London: G. P. Putnam's Sons, 1928. [Includes *The Would-Be Gentleman, Sancho's Master,* and *Dave.*]

151

My First Play. London: Elkin Mathews & Marrot, 1930.
Lady Gregory, Selected Plays. Chosen and arranged by Elizabeth Coxhead. New York: Hill and Wang, 1963.

2. Prose

Arabi and His Household. London: Kegan Paul, Trench & Co.,1882.
Sir William Gregory, K. C. M. G., An Autobiography. Ed. Lady Gregory. London: John Murray, 1894.
Mr. Gregory's Letter-Box. Ed. Lady Gregory. London: Smith, Elder & Co., 1898.
Ideals in Ireland. Ed. Lady Gregory. London: At the Unicorn, 1901.
Cuchulain of Muirthemme. London: John Murray, 1902.
Poets and Dreamers. Dublin: Hodges, Figgis & Co., Ltd., 1903.
Gods and Fighting Men. New York: Charles Scribner's Sons, 1904.
A Book of Saints and Wonders. London: John Murray, 1907.
The Kiltartan Wonder Book. Dublin: Maunsel and Co., Ltd., 1910.
Our Irish Theatre. New York and London: G. P. Putnam's Sons, 1913.
The Kiltartan Poetry Book. New York and London: G. P. Putnam's Sons, 1919.
Visions and Beliefs in the West of Ireland. First and second series (vols. I and II). New York and London: G. P. Putnam's Sons, 1920.
Hugh Lane's Life and Achievement. London: John Murray, 1921.
A Case for the Return of Hugh Lane's Pictures to Dublin. Dublin: The Talbot Press Ltd., 1926.
Coole. Dublin: The Cuala Press, 1931.
Lady Gregory's Journals, 1916–1930. Ed. Lennox Robinson. New York: The Macmillan Company, 1947.
Seventy Years. Ed. Colin Smythe. New York: Macmillan, 1974.

SECONDARY SOURCES

ADAMS, HAZARD. *Lady Gregory*. Lewisburg: Bucknell University Press, 1973. Brief critical analysis; contains several insights into Lady Gregory's works, especially her plays.
AYLING, RONALD. "Charwoman of the Abbey." *The Shaw Review*, IV (September 1961), 7–15. Includes an appreciative assessment of Miss Coxhead's evaluation of Lady Gregory.
BOYD, ERNEST A. *Ireland's Literary Renaissance*. New York: John Lane Company, 1916. Ponderously written but reliable in its description of the Irish Theatre movement's various factions.
BROWN, IVOR. *Shaw in His Time*. London: Thomas Nelson and Sons, Ltd., 1965. Negative picture of Lady Gregory, but the book correctly assesses the political and artistic forces in late nineteenth century Ireland.

BROWN, MALCOLM. *The Politics of Irish Literature, from Thomas Davis to W. B. Yeats*. Seattle: University of Washington Press, 1972. Thorough, readable account of the political forces that influenced writings of the Irish Renaissance.

BUSHRUI, S. B. *Yeats's Verse-Plays: The Revisions, 1900–1910*. Oxford: Clarendon Press, 1965. Scholarly work; demonstrates, in passing, the great influence of Lady Gregory upon Yeats.

COXHEAD, ELIZABETH. *Lady Gregory, A Literary Portrait*. 2nd ed. London: Secker & Warburg, 1966. Key work in Lady Gregory studies; successfully demonstrates thesis that Lady Gregory is an excellent though much neglected writer and literary figure.

DUNLEAVY, GARETH W. *Douglas Hyde*. Lewisburg: Bucknell University Press, 1974. An altogether sound statement concerning Hyde's contribution to Irish letters.

EDWARDS, A. C., ED. "The Lady Gregory Letters to Sean O'Casey." *Modern Drama*, VIII (May 1965), 95–111. Adds little to Lady Gregory's *Journals* but amplifies the fact that her relationship with O'Casey after *The Silver Tassie* was somewhat stiff despite her efforts to revivify their friendship.

ELLIS-FERMOR, UNA. *The Irish Dramatic Movement*. 2nd ed. London: Methuen and Company, Ltd., 1954. Finest analysis of drama written during the Irish Renaissance, but judgment about the worth of individual plays is sometimes subjective.

FALLON, GABRIEL. *Sean O'Casey, the Man I Knew*. London: Routledge & Kegan Paul, 1965. Well-written, reliable firsthand account of the riots over O'Casey's plays; at times, the picture of O'Casey's "martyrdom" is overly sympathetic.

FAY, GERARD. *The Abbey Theatre, Cradle of Genius*. London: Hollis & Carter, 1958. For the most part, an impartial look at personalities behind the scenes during the early days of the Abbey.

FAY, W. G. AND CATHERINE CARSWELL. *The Fays of the Abbey Theatre, An Autobiographical Record*. New York: Harcourt, Brace and Company, 1935. Discursive series of reminiscences; valuable when it demonstrates that Lady Gregory's personality was responsible for making the Irish Theatre at least somewhat palatable to the average Dubliner.

GOGARTY, OLIVER ST. J. *As I Was Going Down Sackville Street*. New York: Reynal & Hitchcock, 1937. Destructive picture of Lady Gregory; contains many unsupported accusations.

HOGAN, ROBERT, AND MICHAEL J. O'NEILL, EDS. *Joseph Holloway's Abbey Theatre, A Selection from His Unpublished Journal, Impressions of a Dublin Playgoer*. Carbondale and Edwardsville: Southern Illinois University Press, 1967. Indispensable book; gives a fair selection from the writing of a man who saw every performance of the Abbey Theatre.

Holloway is generally reliable with details concerning the plays, but very nearsighted in political and artistic judgments.

HONE, JOSEPH. *W. B. Yeats, 1865–1939.* 2nd ed. London: Macmillan and Company, Ltd., 1965. Excellent biography of the poet.

HOWARTH, HERBERT. *The Irish Writers, 1880–1940.* New York: Hill and Wang, 1958. Thought-provoking study of the interrelationship between politics and art; stresses impact of Messiah image upon Irish rebellions.

HYDE, DOUGLAS. *Love Songs of Connacht.* Dublin and Waterford: M. H. Gill & Son, Ltd., 1893. Demonstrates the effectiveness of Gaelic-English as a medium for poetry.

KAVANAUGH, PETER. *The Story of the Abbey Theatre, from Its Origins in 1899 to the Present.* New York: The Devin-Adair Company, 1950. Competent and concise study; neglects Lady Gregory's importance in the theater but stresses Yeats's influence.

KINSELLA, THOMAS, trans. *The Táin.* Dublin: Dolmen Press, 1969. The finest modern version of the *Táin Bó Cuailnge*.

KOPPER, EDWARD A., JR. "Lady Gregory and *Finnegans Wake.*" *A Wake Newslitter*, new series, IX (December 1972), 103–07. Outlines Joyce's use of accounts of Lady Gregory's life and works as sources for parts of the *Wake*.

MALONE, ANDREW E. *The Irish Drama.* New York: Benjamin Blom, Inc., 1965. Competent, general study of the Irish Theatre except for its negative picture of O'Casey; excellent in its analysis of the European and Gaelic influences on the drama.

McHUGH, ROGER. "Sean O'Casey and Lady Gregory." *James Joyce Quarterly*, VIII (Fall 1970), 119–23. Discusses the positive ingredients in the relationships between the two.

MOORE, GEORGE. *Hail and Farewell!* Vol. I. New York: D. Appleton and Company, 1925. More reliable than Gogarty's pronouncements but greatly influenced by Lady Gregory's antagonism to Moore.

MORE, P. E. "The Epic of Ireland." *Shelburne Essays.* First series. New York and London: G. P. Putnam's Sons, 1904. Perceptive, brief statement of the merits and faults of the Irish sagas and of Lady Gregory's adaptations of them.

MURPHY, DANIEL J. "Lady Gregory, Co-author and Sometimes Author of the Plays of W. B. Yeats." Eds. Raymond J. Porter and James D. Brophy. In *Modern Irish Literature: Essays in Honor of William York Tindall*, New Rochelle: Iona College Press, 1972. Interesting observations based upon recent scholarship.

————. "Yeats and Lady Gregory: A Unique Dramatic Collaboration." *Modern Drama*, VIII (December 1964), 322–28. One of the first important examinations of Lady Gregory's influence upon Yeat's style.

O'CASEY, EILEEN. *Sean*. Ed. and introd. by J. C. Trewin. London: Pan Books, Ltd., 1973. Contains excellent background material on *The Silver Tassie* and Lady Gregory's relationship with O'Casey.

O'CASEY, SEAN. *Inishfallen, Fare Thee Well*. New York: The Macmillan Company, 1949. The anecdotes about Lady Gregory are indispensable to an understanding of the humanity of her personality, but O'Casey often draws the wrong inferences from events.

———. *The Sting and the Twinkle*. Eds. E. H. Mikhail and John O'Riordan. New York: Barnes & Noble, 1975. Collection of O'Casey's conversations; contains his famous statement that Lady Gregory was the real genius behind the Irish Theatre movement.

O'FAOLÁIN, SEAN. "Fifty Years of Irish Writing." *Studies*, LI (Spring 1962), 93–105.

PORTER, RAYMOND J. "The Irish Messianic Tradition." *Emory University Quarterly*, XXII (1966), 29–35. Views the works of Yeats and Lady Gregory through the light of Irish myth.

ROBINSON, LENNOX. *Ireland's Abbey Theatre, A History, 1899–1951*. London: Sidgwick and Jackson Limited, 1951. Cumbersome book but contains a great deal of fresh information from unlikely places about the early days of the Abbey.

SADDLEMYER, ANN. *In Defence of Lady Gregory, Playwright*. Dublin: The Dolmen Press, 1966. Views Lady Gregory's works through themes and motifs; presents a number of perceptive points about the plays.

SKELTON, ROBIN, AND ANN SADDLEMYER, eds. *The World of W. B. Yeats, Essays in Perspective*. Victoria, British Columbia: University of Victoria Press, 1965. Traces the effects of the Celtic Revival upon the Irish Renaissance.

TAYLOR, ESTELLA R. *The Modern Irish Writers*. Lawrence: University of Kansas Press, 1954. Discursive but a storehouse of criticism concerning politics during the Irish Renaissance.

THOMPSON, WILLIAM IRWIN. *The Imagination of an Insurrection, Dublin, Easter 1916*. New York: Oxford University Press, 1967. Provocative study of the influence of Irish writers upon the rising.

TOKSVIG, SIGNE. "A Visit to Lady Gregory." *North American Review*, CCXIV (August 1921), 190–200. Characterizes Lady Gregory as a warm person; gives account of the militarism of the times.

TYNAN, KATHERINE. *Twenty-Five Years: Reminiscences*. New York: The Devin-Adair Company, 1913. Excellent account of the Parnell era.

WEYGANDT, CORNELIUS. *Irish Plays and Playwrights*. Boston and New York: Houghton Mifflin Company, 1913. Slightly exaggerates the stature of Lady Gregory's work in Irish myth but does define Lady Gregory's contribution to the folklore movement.

YEATS, W. B. *Autobiographies*. London: Macmillan and Company, Ltd.,

1956. Contains *Dramatis Personae* which accurately records Lady Gregory's family ties and her organizational ability but which omits mention of her playwriting genius.

————*The Celtic Twilight, Men and Women, Dhouls and Faeries.* London: Lawrence and Bullen, 1893. Expresses Yeats's belief in the magic behind the everyday experiences of Irish peasants.

Index